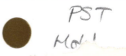
THE NOBLE LIAR

HOW AND WHY THE BBC DISTORTS THE NEWS
TO PROMOTE A LIBERAL AGENDA

THE
NOBLE
LIAR

ROBIN AITKEN

Biteback Publishing

First published in Great Britain in 2018 by
Biteback Publishing Ltd
Westminster Tower
3 Albert Embankment
London SE1 7SP
Copyright © Robin Aitken 2018

Robin Aitken has asserted his right under the Copyright, Designs
and Patents Act 1988 to be identified as the author of this work.

ISBN 978-1-78590-349-6

10 9 8 7 6 5 4 3 2

A CIP catalogue record for this book is available from the British Library.

Set in Minion Pro

Printed and bound in Great Britain by
CPI Group (UK) Ltd, Croydon CR0 4YY

MIX
Paper from
responsible sources
FSC® C020471

CONTENTS

To Sarah, Nancy and Alice, whose love
and support sustain me.

THE STATE WE ARE IN

D EAR READER, INDULGE ME for a few moments and enter into a thought experiment. Suppose you were to land in Britain from outer space, an alien explorer with no foreknowledge of the country, no understanding of its culture or history, how would you go about trying to make sense of the place? A useful place to start might be to try to determine where authority lay. 'Who's in charge here?', the alien wants to know, deploying that intergalactic travel cliché, 'Take me to your leader'. But unravelling the question – what makes this place tick? – yields a very complex answer with many ambiguities and conundrums.

Perhaps our alien would seek out and consult some constitutional expert to guide them through the formal structure.

They might be told that Britain, aka the United Kingdom, is a constitutional monarchy, and that all power is exercised in the name of the monarch. They would hear how the Crown is a hereditary institution, with kingship passed down through the family line; that usually the monarch is male, but can be female if the family tree so dictates. It would then have to be explained that although the monarch is the head of state from whom all authority notionally flows, in reality, the individual sitting on the throne exercises almost no executive power.

Real power, they would learn, lies in the hands of Parliament (and its legislature), which passes laws in the monarch's name; and that Parliament is the domain of people we call politicians, and that these people are elected by the ordinary citizens who, periodically, are asked to vote to elect those they favour. This system, we call 'democracy'. We would have to introduce our visitor to the idea of 'the rule of law', which embodies the important principle that, once Parliament has legislated, everyone in the country is subject to the law – no one is above it – and that this system relies upon an acquiescence by all, even those who oppose certain specific laws.

This explanation, though, is far from comprehensive; to make sense of how democracy works the whole question of political parties would have to be untangled – as well as an elucidation of what 'parties' actually are. Namely, that they are voluntary groupings that coalesce around certain abstract philosophical and economic ideas. We would have to explain that, while all parties are to a certain extent tribes that stick together in the face of opponents, some of the smaller parties, like the Scottish National Party and Plaid Cymru are much more tribal, and are largely concerned with group identity. At some point our constitutional expert would also have to try to outline that the foregoing explanation applies only to the House of Commons, and that, when it comes to the 'Upper Chamber', a whole different set of – sometimes illogical – rules apply. Luckily our alien is equipped with massively powerful cognitive abilities, so all this information can be taken in without trouble; they are, after all, only seeking to understand what the system is – they are not trying to interrogate our constitutionalist expert about any anomalies or inconsistencies.

So, Parliament, democracy and the rule of law succinctly explained, there we have it: that is where authority lies in contemporary Britain. Not so fast, alien truth seeker. We have many levels of complexity yet to unravel. There is, for instance, the European Union, and its authority superimposed on our domestic arrangements. It is true, we seem to be on our way out of that particular structure, but there are other international organisations of which the UK is a member, which can also lay claim to some authority in certain areas of life. The UN, NATO, the International Court of Justice, and so on: a whole host of organisations which can exercise some degree of authority. And then there are referendums – those occasional plebiscites that test the public will on matters of importance.

And so our visitor would come to see that though pre-eminent, Parliament's authority is not absolute. And at this point, it would have to be explained that the account given so far only covers the formal structures of power. To understand why that power is exercised in the way it is we would have to introduce our alien visitor to another concept, which we might term moral authority. That is to say, the authority which flows from our understanding of fundamental truth. A grasp of this particular concept is necessary to comprehend why the politicians who we elect do what they do; and to understand the mechanisms by which the legislature is guided, so that it is in accord with the popular will. So, for instance, we hold it to be a fundamental truth that no individual can be executed by the state because we have decided that it is always wrong for the state to kill its own citizens. But from where does such a belief come? Not from the popular will, which has always been in favour of the death penalty; although support for the death penalty has been slowly declining and dipped below 50 per cent for the first time in 2015, according to recent figures. And if you discount the undecided, those wanting its reintroduction out-number opponents by 45 per cent to 39 per cent. So, answering this question introduces a level of complexity quite above and beyond anything which our back-of-the-envelope introductory course on the British constitution has so far attempted.

From where does this moral authority derive? Our alien quite understandably wants to know. Where to start? Perhaps with Christianity and the 'national church' – the Church of England – and some elementary theology. At this point our alien would have to be introduced to the notion of an omniscient Creator who we call God; an entity beyond human understanding who brought our planet, and indeed the whole universe including our alien, into being through an act of inscrutable will at the beginning of the dimension we call time. One can foresee some potential problems here, but let us battle on regardless (we aren't inviting a debating contest with this stranger, merely telling it how it is according to orthodox Christian teaching): God has handed down to us fundamental truths which, should we listen to our consciences, will guide our actions. But then we would have to heavily qualify this belief by explaining that the Church of England, though nominally the 'national church', has only a relatively small and dwindling number of members. And that, in fact, in the UK there are many other religions, some of which have significantly more committed adherents than the C. of E.

Our alien might, at this point, be forgiven for some confusion; after all, surely the 'national church' of which the monarch is the 'supreme governor' has some right to assert primacy in this area? The point could be argued, but not conclusively. There is no clear answer. And anyway, we would be obliged to point out that, according to polling evidence, many citizens reject this traditional idea of a Creator God along with the right of any of the many and various churches to lay claim to any moral authority whatsoever. Many Britons see themselves as secularists – actively opposed to religion of all stripes – and if one had to pigeonhole their philosophy, 'humanism' might be as good a label as any.

So what moral authority do these citizens, the atheists, acknowledge? Well, that is a devilishly tricky question to answer. We would have to admit that many citizens have but little faith in the moral authority of politicians but that – by way of counterbalance – there is widespread support for the notion of 'the rule of law'. While many citizens are critical of the law as it stands, and believe it should be improved in ways that accord with their own preferences (so that there is a constant debate about what the law should be), the United Kingdom is a country where there is a consensus that the law binds us all. Leaving aside criminals, who obviously reject the law, here perhaps we have arrived on solid ground. It is in the law itself that true authority resides, and the fact that our laws derive from a democratic process invests them with a kind of moral authority. But our alien is puzzled; what, it wants to know, determines what the law should be? The politicians, our expert replies, who take their instruction from the voters. And how do the voters form their view of what the law should be? Ah, now we have hit upon a further complexity.

The voters formulate their views of how the world should

be through their own intellectual processes, which in turn, are informed by a myriad of sources; everything from a conversation with a neighbour over the hedge (a quaint image – more likely these days to be a Facebook exchange), to their own reading and investigation of issues important to them, as well as following formal political debates accommodated by newspapers, radio, television and online sources. These interactions between individuals and the ideas floating around them are what the commentators, somewhat pompously, call the 'national conversation' – though it seems most of the time, most people are not included. It is a conversation heavily mediated by various forms of communication – books, newspapers, radio, television, the internet – doubtless all rather primitive in the view of this advanced alien. This debate, unceasingly conducted through all the different types of media available and contributed to by many different individuals and organisations, acts upon the politicians who then enact laws to carry into effect the will of the majority. Simple, *n'est-ce pas*?

Our alien visitor, because of their superior cognition, has easily grasped the main points; they get our drift. They see that, in theory at least, in the UK, the voters are the masters: authority flows from the people, upwards, to Parliament, which enacts the will of the people by passing laws that reflect the majority view. They understand that this is an imperfect system in the sense that it means no one individual is ever completely satisfied with the state of the law (because it is unlikely that any one individual agrees with every law), but that this collective expression of the majority's preferences – what we call public opinion – is a serviceable starting point for ruling the country according to the will of the people. It does not then take our alien long to figure out that the most important influence acting on the whole democratic mechanism is this notion of the public's aggregate opinion; if the system is working properly, a majority opinion emerges in the public mind and the legislators duly take notice and pass laws accordingly. And it follows from this that the institutions which mould public opinion play a very important role in the whole process. The ideal situation is that through a process of public debate everyone engages with a topic, the different sides struggle for supremacy and eventually one side emerges triumphant having persuaded a majority to support it. Then this winning idea is transmitted via the various mechanisms which act upon the legislators and, at the end of the process, new laws and regulations emerge reflecting the majority opinion. But is this, in reality, how our system works?

At this point our explanation needs to take a short detour to describe the country's media landscape. The UK is a country rich in media sources. We have about 100 daily newspapers: some national, some regional, and about 450 weekly newspapers. There are also about 8,000 magazine titles, of which some are very specialist, but about 3,000 of which are aimed at a general audience (an increasing number are available only online). We have an enormously prolific book publishing industry – the UK publishes about 180,000 books per year,[1] which is the highest, per capita, in the world. We also have nearly 500 television stations, which variously cater for both a broad range of tastes as well more niche markets, and there are about 600 radio stations. And, finally, there's the internet, where the range and variety of sources cannot reliably be counted. What this amounts to is a cornucopia of information; we are surrounded by a sea of data, factual news reports and opinion. No one in Britain can plausibly claim to be starved of facts – seek and ye shall find.

Given all this our alien might conclude that the UK has the wherewithal to nourish a system that reliably reflects the popular will, and, in theory, that is the case. But if our alien, having absorbed the theory, set about doing some fieldwork among the natives, they would find that is not how it seems to an increasing number of citizens. Rather, the country appears at odds with itself over all manner of subjects. Our alien would discover that in the view of many people, the rules which govern our lives make no sense any longer; that there is a deep

---

1 The most recent figures available are from 2013 when the International Publishers Association recorded that 184,000 new and revised titles were published. This equates to 2,857 titles per million inhabitants, placing the UK an astonishing 1,000 plus titles ahead of second-placed Taiwan. The US was considerably lower, at 959 titles per million.

disconnect between the views of the ordinary citizen, based on their own 'common sense', and the prevailing orthodoxies which are promoted in the media and which often end up being enshrined in legislation. Many people feel something has gone wrong.

Thankfully, you might feel, we can now discard the rather tiresome device of our alien and bring the subject of this book into focus: it is an examination of why there is such a gulf between the world as the media presents it, and the world as most ordinary people experience it. Why is it that so many people find no echo of their own opinions in the big media outlets that serve them? And this brings the British Broadcasting Corporation to centre stage. The BBC, by a very large margin, is the most important media organisation in the country, and to understand what has gone wrong, we need to examine this mighty institution in close detail.

This book is about something so pervasive that it is difficult to see it clearly. It is like the story of the three fish. Two fish were swimming side by side in their pond; a third fish swam towards them and as he passed said, 'Nice water today', and swam on. After he'd gone, one of the fish turned to his companion and said, 'What's water?' The mass media is the water we swim in and it takes an effort of concentration to see it as it really is. The etymology of the word 'media' leads back to its Latin root, meaning 'intermediate agency'. In our common usage it implies all those intermediate agencies, like the BBC, which present us with information about the world. It is a function so commonplace that we hardly notice it, and yet it has a profound impact on the way we live. Without an understanding of its guiding philosophy we are in danger of being led blindfold into a way of thinking we have not freely chosen, but have merely absorbed.

In pursuit of better understanding our media, and particularly the BBC, the following pages will explore the size, scope and influence of the Corporation within the context of issues of contemporary importance; Brexit, for instance. The writer and social commentator David Goodhart coined a useful formula for a difference in outlook between two big groups in society; he said that people are largely divided into 'somewheres' and 'anywheres'. His theory is that 'somewheres' are more traditional types: the sort of people who feel rooted in a particular place in a particular culture. These are the sort of people who voted to leave the EU. 'Anywheres', by contrast, are the kind of people who feel pretty much at home anywhere in the Western world; these are the global citizens who feel as much at ease in Sydney, Saratoga or Sydenham. They have wider horizons and weaker national allegiances and they voted instinctively to remain in the EU. One of the things this book examines is why it has come to be that the BBC – which might be thought quintessentially British – so often sounds like one of these 'anywheres'.

If my analysis is right, an understanding the BBC's 'deep state' helps to explain certain obvious biases in its news coverage;

why it is, for instance, that the Corporation is so nakedly hostile to Donald Trump's presidency and Viktor Orbán's ascendancy in Hungary. Also, why the theories that drive radical feminism are never challenged and why the difficult subject of Islam in the West is consistently soft-pedalled. Most importantly, and overarchingly, this book explains how it is that the BBC has become so deeply hostile to social conservatism – that way of thinking, shared by tens of millions of us, which values a traditional moral code that emphasises virtues like patriotism, self-restraint and decency. Social conservatives are at odds with a media culture which is obsessed with identity politics; they mistrust the campaigns of self-declared victimised minorities – whether defined by sexual orientation, gender or ethnicity.

The BBC has come to the point where it now, seemingly automatically, takes the side of the identitarians in every debate. It has become an unthinking champion of a set of values sometimes called 'liberal' (but in no way distinguished by the tolerance once thought integral to a liberal mindset), which has profoundly changed British society over the past half-century. The culture we inhabit – much of it trashy, tawdry and shallow – is in large measure the creation of our media. Individually, we have not willed this culture into existence, it is the work of many hands, but it has arrived nevertheless because there has been no apparent way to stop it, nor any concerted attempt to do so. The first step in reversing the process is for us to collectively understand it, which is precisely what this book sets out to achieve.

The title of this book draws on a concept originated in Plato's *Republic*; a 'noble lie' is a myth or an untruth, knowingly propagated by an elite, in order to promote and maintain social harmony or advance an agenda. The BBC prides itself on being a 'truth teller': its hard-won, worldwide reputation is built on the foundation stone of audience trust. But what 'truth' is the BBC telling? It is the contention of this book that the BBC, along with its media and establishment allies, has become the vehicle for the propagation of a series of noble lies in pursuit of a political agenda.

Though the noble lie is always told with the best of intentions, there is an inherent problem with it: the deception misleads people and substitutes imagined problems for real ones. The great danger is that sooner or later people will realise they have been duped, and this will be a moment of great peril for the established order – with unpredictable consequences. This is the prospect facing Britain. What is urgently needed, this book will argue, is a new and bracing honesty which allows the nation to face its problems in full possession of some uncomfortable facts.

CHAPTER ONE

LOOK WHO'S IN THE BULLY PULPIT

I F YOU TAKE A WALK from Fleet Street, along the Embankment to Millbank, which lies just beyond the Palace of Westminster, you trace the route of a migration of media power which has occurred over the past fifty years. Back then, in the 1960s, it was the great newspaper titles that wielded media clout. Though most of us didn't recognise it at the time, the 1960s were the beginning of the end of the golden age of print journalism. At the time, titles like the *Daily Express*, the *Daily Telegraph*, the *Mirror* and *The Times* then still made the political weather. But the writing was on the wall, or rather, the screen. Already by this point the broadcasters were growing in confidence, and the print media's position as the most powerful conduit of public opinion was under sustained challenge. The burgeoning confidence of television was welcomed by some, particularly those who had always resented and criticised the power of the newspapers. Those papers, naturally enough, reflected the views of their proprietors; and those proprietors, in the main, turned out to be forceful (sometimes unscrupulous) capitalists. The left in the '60s quickly, and presciently, identified television as a powerful counterweight to a predominantly right-wing press.

Today Fleet Street is a shadow of its former self both in terms of political power and commercial heft; though most of the old titles still exist, like gentlefolk fallen on hard times they live in reduced circumstances and no longer count for so much in the wider world. Their share of influence has dwindled while that of the broadcasters, and now the online news sites, has grown ever stronger. A quick foray into newspaper circulation figures bears this out. In 1950, in a country where there were about 15 million households, the number of daily papers sold was around 21 million, but on Sundays an extraordinary 31 million. So in those days, on average, every household was consuming more than one daily paper and two on Sundays.

By comparison, in 2010, there were some 25 million households, but only 10 million daily and about 10 million Sunday papers were sold: so only two out of every five households were reading a daily or Sunday paper. No figure better illustrates the dramatic decline of the newspaper reading habit.[1] It is true that some papers still have the power, occasionally, to terrify and cow the politicians, but newspaper journalists are well aware that the glory days are past. The power has been dispersed both physically (the newspaper trade no longer has an identifiable district) and metaphorically – there are now many more competitors for the political influence that was once the sole preserve of print journalism.

Probably few people, except newspapermen themselves, mourn the loss of influence and the way that power has seeped from the printed to the spoken word. The process, anyway, was a natural consequence of technological advance. One hundred years ago broadcasting barely existed and the technology it relied upon was cumbersome; by comparison, newspaper production was then a state-of-the-art technology enabling the most successful titles to run off millions of copies daily and efficiently distribute them to every corner of the kingdom. Today, no print technology can compete in terms of speed and ease of distribution with broadcasters and the internet; the newspapers have had to content themselves with a dwindling and ageing audience. They have learned to concentrate their efforts on those areas where they have a remaining competitive advantage: in the upmarket titles this means investigative

---

1 See: http://media-cmi.com/downloads/Sixty_Years_Daily_Newspaper_Circulation_Trends_050611.pdf

journalism and intelligent opinion pieces, while among the red tops, entertaining celebrity gossip and sensationalism are their remaining strengths. So the newspapers eke out an existence in changed circumstances – but the age of the press baron who could make governments tremble is surely past, and the power they once wielded has been shared out among others.

Some, particularly on the left, celebrate this phenomenon. One of the most wearisome tropes of the British left is that of the 'Tory press', which is blamed for the failure of the movement to seize power as often as its supporters feel it deserves. It is a striking fact that in the past 100 years there have been only roughly thirty years of Labour rule – thirteen of those under the now-reviled centrist Tony Blair and his successor, Gordon Brown – and many on the left put a large part of the blame for that on the influence of our daily newspapers. This is a convenient, albeit lame, excuse, because it shifts the blame from the failure of the left to win the political argument onto the shoulders of wicked press barons. And it doesn't really stand up to scrutiny, because it ignores the fact that the left has always had its own, ultra-loyal newspaper supporters, and that when the left offers popular, moderate, policies – as Tony Blair did in 1997 – some newspapers (most significantly in that year, Rupert Murdoch's *The Sun*) are prepared to switch sides. That aside, broadcasting has proved to be much more congenial to the left, and the left's dominance of the airwaves has had profound consequences. Whether or not the transfer of power from print to broadcast should be celebrated or regretted will depend on personal political preference, but there can be no doubting its reality.

Much has been written in recent years about the fragmentation of the media market in Britain (not that this is an exclusively British phenomenon – the same forces have been at work in every major market across the globe). And it is undoubtedly true that beginning in the 1980s, new players started to appear in Western media markets. The pace of change accelerated through subsequent decades beginning with cable TV in the US, which allowed niche services to emerge to challenge the previously dominant networks; then came satellite broadcasters like Sky, which provided yet more competition and, finally, when the internet came of age, a multitude of providers sprang up, exploiting the near-limitless possibilities of the digital world.

It was technological advance that drove this revolution. The key thing to understand is that, in contrast to the early days of broadcasting when there was a finite resource (i.e. the spectrum of wavelengths which could be utilised), in the era of the internet there is virtually no limit at all to the number of broadcasters who can make an offering to the public. And along with this limitless platform is the other, hugely significant fact, that entry costs have also fallen precipitously, so that one bright young thing with one bright young idea can build a media presence from a standing start – something simply impossible in the era of Big Print.

It is salutary to remember that back in the early years of the twentieth century European governments agreed by treaty which country should be given which wavelength, so that the broadcasts of each country shouldn't interfere with its neighbours'; it meant that radio frequencies were treated like fish stocks and divided up accordingly.[2] In practice, that meant there was a very small number of broadcasting organisations and these were usually state-controlled. The contrast today is striking. First, cable (which started on a small scale in the 1950s), then satellite in the '60s, then digital opened up nearly unlimited horizons for broadcasters and the idea of rationing or constraining the number of providers now seems quaint. But what is also remarkable is how, despite the digital revolution, the traditional British broadcasters, and in particular the BBC, have met the challenge and maintained their position.

In this sense the established UK broadcasters have defied the pundits. Dazzled by the pace of technological change, the death of traditional TV has been much foretold, and has become a staple of commentaries on the changing broadcasting landscape. Such commentaries are often tinged with regret;

---

2 In 1926 radio engineers from around Europe gathered in Geneva to hammer out an agreement which resulted in a European treaty to govern who could use what part of the radio spectrum for national broadcasting.

the writer looks back to a golden age when the population was united by the shared experience of television. In that time a single programme – usually entertainment, but sometimes a factual documentary – would be watched, simultaneously (as this was an era when few people could record or 'time shift' programmes) by a significant proportion of the entire population. Such programmes became the staple of the following days' conversation, and the whole shared experience became an important part of the national consciousness. That happens much less frequently today because of the explosion of outlets: there have been individual gains (more consumer choice), but a collective loss (less shared experience). And yet, in spite of it all, the BBC still triumphantly bestrides the British media scene.

Here are some numbers, all culled from the BBC's 2017/18 annual report: 92 per cent of UK adults use a BBC service at least once a week and 80 per cent of UK adults consume BBC news each week; BBC online is browsed by 30 million unique UK users weekly and 51.5 per cent of UK adults are regular users; 80 per cent of people watch some BBC TV each week and the Corporation's overall share of TV viewing is 32 per cent. What these figures show – and there are reams of others which also underline how ubiquitous the BBC has become – is that the organisation has successfully consolidated its position at the heart of national life at a time when the competition has never been so fierce. There is no other organisation, in any sphere of national life, not the NHS, nor any agency of government, which touches so many of us so directly and so often as the BBC. What is more, there is often an intimacy about this relationship compared to most others: we invite the BBC into our living rooms, our kitchens, our bathrooms and bedrooms. From dawn to dusk, like our guardian angels, the Corporation is there at our side. Perhaps because of this ubiquity the BBC scores highly on trust, with 57 per cent of people saying they put their faith in it compared to other main news providers.[3] That might sound a slightly underwhelming figure until you learn that the next most trusted source scores a measly 10 per cent. Despite all the problems of recent years – among them inflated salaries, the gender pay gap, and worst of all the Jimmy Savile scandal – the BBC has weathered the storm in pretty good shape and still, seemingly, commands the affection and trust of the nation. And not just this nation: worldwide the BBC has a weekly audience of 372 million people, and is often a more trusted source of information than indigenous broadcasters. On this measure the BBC is the UK's most important cultural export by a very large margin.

What these statistics underline is the central position that the BBC holds in the UK's media landscape. In any debate about media plurality in the UK the BBC is the elephant in

---

3 See: https://downloads.bbc.co.uk/aboutthebbc/insidethebbc/howwework/
   reports/pdf/bbc_report_trust_and_impartiality_nov_2017.pdf

the room. And yet, when the subject periodically surfaces, it is almost never about the BBC at all; in fact, in recent decades debate has focused, almost exclusively, on Rupert Murdoch's media enterprises. But any disinterested observer would surely find this peculiar; Murdoch, it is true, owns a stable of powerful newspapers – *The Sun* (which, though steadily declining, still has the highest circulation of all UK dailies), *The Times* and the *Sunday Times* – but his share of the television market is a modest 8.3 per cent, and his radio presence (since June 2016 Murdoch has owned Wireless Group which is the parent company of Talksport and Talkradio and some UK local radio franchises) is small, albeit growing. But Murdoch is a controversial figure, with many powerful enemies particularly, but not exclusively, on the left; that is why his media empire gets such close scrutiny while there is very little questioning of the BBC's market dominance. The BBC gets a pass because most people take it for granted that it is a benign influence; in contrast, Murdoch's motives are always suspect. Some of this doubtless dates back to the premiership of Margaret Thatcher; Murdoch was her stalwart supporter – and some people have never forgiven him for it.

Another aspect of the BBC which deserves mention is its finances. The bulk of the BBC's income comes from the annual licence fee set at £150.50 that is paid by every householder in the UK who owns a television. That raised £3,787,000,000 in 2017 and in addition the BBC enjoyed further revenue of

£1,167,000,000 through programme sales overseas. So the BBC's total income for this period was just shy of £5 billion. To most people that might sound like quite a lot of money, but the Corporation's cheerleaders argue that, in the reality of today's global media market, it is pretty small beer. In the spring of 2016, two years after he stood down as chairman of the BBC Trust, Lord Patten, the former Tory politician Chris Patten, made a ringing endorsement of the current financial settlement for the BBC. Here is part of what he said:

> We need to say the things about the BBC that its many commercial enemies would prefer you not to know. Things they won't report tomorrow if they cover this speech at all. Like the fact that the BBC's real income has fallen over the past decade by more than 15 per cent. Like the fact that in the past five years alone BSkyB's revenues went up by more than 16 per cent, and ITV's increased by 21 per cent. Like the fact that the BBC, once a giant in the communications market, is as the House of Lords Select Committee on Communications recently argued, 'a comparatively small player', now dwarfed by multinational platforms who drive up the cost of content – of acquisition, of talent, of production, and of ideas – but have no interest in the UK except as a market. Like the fact that this supposedly fat-cat BBC keeps losing key executives because rivals offer twice the salaries. And this supposedly bloated, top-heavy,

bureaucratic BBC now has its overheads down to just 7.6 per cent – way, way below the public sector average of 11.2.[4]

Lord Patten comes from that wing of the Tory Party that likes to style itself as 'one nation'. His political glory days were in the early 1990s when, as chairman of the party under Prime Minister John Major, he was an important figure right at the heart of government. But at the 1992 general election the voters of Bath unceremoniously dumped him and from then on he filled a series of establishment roles, and to start with he landed the plum of last Governor of Hong Kong.[5] In 1998 Tony Blair asked him to oversee the Independent Commission on Policing for Northern Ireland which reported in 1999 and was an important plank in the province's peace settlement. Perhaps by way of a thank-you he was then appointed as one of the UK's two European Commissioners – he was given the external relations brief. In 2003 he was elected as Chancellor of Oxford University (his old alma mater) and then, in 2005, he was elevated to the peerage as Lord Patten of Barnes. It was in 2011 that the chairmanship of the BBC Trust came his way

---

4   Chris Patten, speech given at the Reuters Institute of Journalism, Oxford, 3 May 2016.

5   Chris Patten was appointed Governor of Hong Kong in 1992 and served in that role until the handover to Communist China in 1997. He fulfilled the role with some distinction, standing up for the democratic rights of the Hong Kongers; while his efforts were largely unsuccessful, no one could say he didn't try.

– perhaps the peachiest of all the glittering prizes available to the top rung of the British establishment, and one that capped a stellar career of public service. He certainly proved to be a doughty champion of the Corporation.

In the above speech he rattled the collection plate for an organisation that he saw threatened by the parsimony and ill will of some elements of Prime Minister David Cameron's Tory-dominated coalition government. The speech was replete with references to those who, as Lord Patten saw it, pose a danger to an organisation he believes represents the very best of British:

> A former colleague noted the other day the tiny handful of elected representatives whose rent-a-quote swipes at the BBC guarantee them a mention day after day in a sympathetic press, and he posed the question: where are these constituencies where the voters worry more about the BBC than they do about having a job, or getting a home, or putting food on the plate? I can tell you the answer: they don't exist. No one actually lives there. Like Old Sarum, they are rotten boroughs with grandiloquent names. Old Murdoch; Great Dacre-upon-Thames; Lesser Desmond.[6]

Patten's reading of the situation of the BBC's finances, and thus its effectiveness as a broadcaster, is imperilled by a vengeful

---

6   Chris Patten, op. cit.

clique of right-wing individuals who serve the interests of no one but themselves. What he chooses to ignore is the fact that the licence fee gives the BBC a huge advantage over other media organisations. Unlike its competitors, the BBC does not have to struggle in a fierce competitive environment to earn every pound; instead it gets its income, by law, from every household, in a poll tax by any other name, and one that is hypothecated to sustain a specific service. This gives the organisation absolute certainty about next year's revenue, which endows it with a unique financial stability allowing it to plan expenditure in a way its rivals cannot.

It is true that the BBC's financial settlement has been squeezed in recent years, but it has largely itself to blame for that: the scandalously lavish salaries enjoyed by the BBC's senior executives in the noughties led to a furious backlash from politicians and the public. In the aftermath of the financial crisis of 2008, the £816,000 annual salary of the Director-General, Mark Thompson, alongside the fact that more than fifty BBC executives enjoyed salaries in excess of the Prime Minister's (then £190,000) proved toxic in an economic environment where many ordinary citizens were suffering. The Corporation's top brass were shown up as greedy salarymen who had turned public service into self-service; the episode also seriously damaged BBC staff morale, throwing into stark relief the disparity between what the favoured few paid themselves and average staff salaries, which have never been particularly generous.

Lord Patten was speaking a few months before the fateful referendum on British membership of the EU, and it is no coincidence that the other media organisations he names as 'enemies' of the BBC are all to a greater or lesser degree sceptical of the benefits of British membership. And that is the key to understanding Lord Patten's ire: he has been a lifelong, and passionate, supporter of British membership of the EU and those outlets – like the *Daily Mail* and *The Sun* – which take a different view of the matter are thus his (and by extension the BBC's) enemies. In his autobiography *First Confession*, he could not have been clearer on the matter. He writes:

> The Brexit vote in the UK and the election of President Trump in the USA have together threatened to destroy the foundations of the world order to which my political life, both at home and abroad, has been devoted.[7]

It is worth dwelling on Lord Patten's politics in some detail, because doing so allows us to position him, and the BBC itself, more precisely on the British political spectrum. This is not uncontested territory: the BBC and its apologists have consistently rejected the validity of such an approach. They argue that the BBC cannot be pigeon holed because, bound by its charter obligations, it is an impartial news organisation which

---

7   Chris Patten, *First Confession: A Sort of Memoir* (Allen Lane, 2017), p. 240.

stands out with – and above – the political fray. But this pious fiction is merely an attempt to disguise an underlying truth: the BBC is a profoundly political organisation, and denying this obvious fact is an insult to our intelligence. In fact, many of the BBC's own journalists know BBC reality is different from BBC theory, and have done their bit in demolishing the myth of BBC impartiality: here's Jeremy Paxman, for instance, speaking at the Cheltenham Literary Festival in 2017:

> If you asked me what the politics of most people at the BBC are I should say most people voted Remain, that most people were Labour/Liberal Democrat. I should say that by and large they were liberal with a small 'l' on social issues. I should say that they were people who detested certain kinds of right-wing behaviour.

The BBC, for understandable reasons, could never openly acknowledge the truth of this observation, for to do so would be to undermine the Corporation's raison d'être. But by identifying, in the way he did, the BBC's 'enemies', Lord Patten highlights another, often misunderstood aspect of the BBC – that it is not a passive bystander in the UK's media world, but rather an aggressively self-interested outfit which, when necessary, plays rough. The best recent illustration of this was the way it behaved over the Leveson Inquiry which opened in the autumn of 2011. This judicial inquiry set out to investigate, in forensic detail, the wrongdoings of tabloid journalists working for Rupert Murdoch and others. It transpired that for years Murdoch papers (in particular the *News of the World*, but excluding *The Times*) had been running stories about celebrities and politicians based on information illegally acquired through phone hacking. One of the surprises to emerge was the ease with which this was done: it was, apparently, child's play for journalists to get into the text messages of well-known individuals that gave access to a rich vein of often scurrilous stories about the people involved. It transpired that most of the Fleet Street tabloids were up to the same tricks, but Leveson concentrated on the misdeeds of the Murdoch papers (and it was only years later that the Mirror Group was found to have been guilty of the same practice on a huge scale, which resulted in them having to pay out colossal damages to the wronged individuals).

For the BBC, Leveson was a story it simply couldn't get enough of. Day after day, on its main TV and radio bulletins, the latest revelation from the Royal Courts of Justice led the news in a manner that always seemed disproportionate; after all, the issue at the centre of the affair – journalists breaking communication law in pursuit of gossipy stories about celebrities – hardly warranted top billing in a world where many more important things were happening.

This is not to say that there weren't real abuses by the tabloid press: it is clearly wrong to intercept and publish people's private communications. Some of the episodes, like the *News of the World*'s accessing of the murdered school girl Milly Dowler's phone messages, betrayed a lack of simple human decency (even if the allegations, first made in *The Guardian*, that the *News of the World* journalists had deliberately deleted Milly's messages, later turned out to be wholly false). But that aside, many people saw the Leveson Inquiry as an over-blown episode, driven by rich and entitled celebrities who were only too happy to cooperate with the tabloids when it suited them, but who squealed loudly when things to their disadvantage were published. What is more, there was a very clear political agenda which aimed to extend privacy law to prevent disclosures by the press and subject all newspapers to a state-backed regulator. Such an outcome would have suited some powerful interests very well, at the cost of further restricting the ability of newspapers to uncover wrongdoing. However, little of this counterbalancing narrative made its way into the BBC's wall-to-wall coverage of the wickedness of the Murdoch press.

Why should this have been? Simple: it was settling old scores; the Murdoch press is no friend of the BBC. It keeps a very close eye on everything that happens within the Corporation and highlights failings, whenever it finds them – with manage-ment, finances or ethics. Sadly, for the BBC, there have been many such stories over recent years. Murdoch's justification is that the BBC, as a publicly funded institution, is fair game for journalistic scrutiny. But it goes far beyond that: Murdoch has his own commercial interests at heart and, by undermining the BBC (and in particular its funding mechanism), he can improve the prospects of his own media empire.

Leveson was payback time for the BBC and it made the most of the opportunity. It is very doubtful that the general public ever saw the issue as being as important as BBC news editors did, but that hardly mattered. This time, it was personal, and there was a strong whiff of schadenfreude within the BBC when Murdoch admitted defeat and closed the worst transgressor, the *News of the World*. The BBC had drawn blood and its enemy was seriously wounded. The whole Leveson episode gives us a window into the secret corporate soul of the BBC. And if, as Lord Patten says 'Murdoch' (i.e. *The Sun* and *The Times*), 'Dacre' (the *Daily Mail* titles) and 'Desmond' (the *Express* titles) are the BBC's enemies, it raises the question: who are their 'friends'? Answer that, and it becomes much simpler to understand the internal political culture of the BBC.

The British media landscape is a rich and diverse habitat with thousands of creatures, great and small, but the following analysis will confine itself only to the major players. The first difficulty is to decide on how best to classify organisations in a political sense. The conventional left–right categorisation as originally understood is of only limited use, because it dates from a time when the main determinant of a newspaper's political stance was where it stood on the economic argument.

Post-1945, this was all about public versus private ownership (there were other issues, of course, but economics was the central battleground) and, according to this classification, one could say that *The Guardian*, *The Observer*, the *Mirror* titles and the *Sunday People* were essentially on the left, while the *Telegraph*, the *Financial Times*, the *Mail* and the *Express* titles were on the right. *The Times* was a bit different; at the 1945 election it took a detached stance, though in subsequent elections in the '50s, '60s and '70s it tended to back the Tories. When, in 1981, Rupert Murdoch acquired *The Times*, the paper's editorial stance became more obviously right wing and strongly supported Margaret Thatcher. However, *The Times* has always been the paper of the establishment and tends to gravitate towards whoever is in power – so it was that during the Blair years it generally threw its weight behind New Labour.

There are other newspapers that deserve a mention – *The Independent*, for instance, which came into being in 1986 precisely to break free of the left–right straitjacket. It proclaimed itself as a paper of the centre ground, free from political bias, and, to that end, often supported Liberal Democrat policies, but as it matured it swung more to the left. By the time of the London mayoral election in 2008, it supported the Green Party candidate as its first choice, with the veteran hard leftist Ken Livingstone as its second choice (to no avail, as it turned out, for it was the Tory Boris Johnson who won). An Ipsos MORI poll for the 2010 election estimated that 44 per cent of *Independent* readers voted Lib Dem, 32 per cent voted Labour and only 14 per cent voted Tory. But in the noughties *The Independent* mislaid its recipe for success and by 2016 it ceased existence in its printed form and became an online presence only, where its current orientation seems to be, broadly speaking, centre-left.

In addition to the newspapers, there are a small number of political weeklies which are an important ingredient in the UK media mix; the *New Statesman* has long been seen as the house magazine of the British intellectual left, while *The Spectator* performs the same role on the right. And then there's *The Economist*, which adopts a modified Keynesian orthodoxy on the economic front (Free trade? Absolutely. Public spending? Good and necessary – but not too much of it, please.) while adopting a liberal and progressive stance on other issues; currently the magazine's position seems to embrace a lukewarm centre-left stance with economic caveats.

From the 1990s onwards, until the arrival of Jeremy Corbyn as Labour leader, the divide over economic policy became less pronounced because Labour dropped its constitutional commitment to public ownership (the 'Clause Four' reforms) and, for public consumption at least, reconciled itself to a market economy. There are commentators who say that this point marked the end of left versus right as a useful measure of political allegiance, but that is to misunderstand human nature itself. As Gilbert and Sullivan had it in *Iolanthe*:

I often think it's comical
How nature do contrive,
That every boy and every gal,
that's born into the world alive,
is either a little Liberal,
or else a little Conservative.

There is now a significant body of psychological research which backs up this witty observation on the human condition. In 1969 two pioneering psychologists, Jack and Jeanne Block at the University of California at Berkeley devised an experiment which involved observing the character traits of nursery school children. They broke these down into categories like 'uncomfortable with uncertainty', 'quiet neat and compliant' or 'autonomous and expressive' and 'self-assertive'. They put these observations on ice for two decades and then did a follow-up study on the political opinions of the now young adults in their mid-twenties. And, sure enough, there was a surprisingly high correlation between the traits observed in the young children and the young adults they had become; the 'quiet and neat' girls were much more conservative in outlook than their more self-assertive sisters. The Blocks' research was some of the earliest in what later became a fashionable area of psychological research – how our genetic make-up colours our political world view.

The foregoing is only by way of challenging the assertion, made by some, that one cannot usefully classify political opinions on a left–right continuum. What the Blocks seem to have discovered is that there is a real difference in outlook which broadly divides humankind into two groups – whether one calls that left–right or not. And in the contemporary context, what needs to be understood is that the left–right battleground has shifted off to other territory. The big divide today is not between Keynesians and monetarists – that debate was more or less settled in the 1980s – but between social conservatives and social liberals. That this is the case has been borne out of polling conducted after the Brexit vote, which indicated that how an individual voted in the EU referendum showed a strong correlation to the view they took of social issues. Professor John Curtice of the University of Strathclyde, the doyen of British psephologists, articulated it thusly in an article for *Prospect* magazine:

> The debate about Brexit does not follow the usual contours of British politics. These are usually delineated by the distinction between 'left' and 'right,' between those who want a bit more government in order to make Britain more equal, and those who want a little less state activity so that entrepreneurs are encouraged to stimulate economic growth. Those on the left tend to be inclined to vote Labour, those on the right to back the Conservatives.
>
> However, whether someone was 'left-wing' or 'right-wing' made virtually no difference to how they voted in the EU referendum.

Rather, that ballot was marked by a division between social liberals and social conservatives—that is, between those who are comfortable living in a socially, ethnically and linguistically diverse society and those who place greater emphasis on the need for social cohesion and adherence to common rules and practices. Social liberals tended to vote Remain, social conservatives for Leave.[8]

Now that the debate over economics has been somewhat eclipsed (though the Corbynite left seems determined that there should, once again, be clear water between left and right on the economy) other social issues are a better way of classifying individuals – and organisations. How 'liberal' or 'conservative' one is on a social issue like transgenderism, or multiculturalism, is now a better indicator of political allegiance. And this yardstick can be usefully applied to the media: *The Guardian*, for instance, is hyper-socially liberal, while the *Daily Mail* is much more conservative on these issues. *The Times* is socially liberal – often stridently so – as is the *Financial Times*. *The Economist* is very definitely at the liberal end of the spectrum. Here, for instance, is its social policy editor, Emma Duncan, writing in *The Times* about attitudes to Brexit:

---

8 John Curtice, 'After Brexit, it's no longer about "left" and "right" – it's now social liberals vs social conservatives', *Prospect* magazine, 18 December 2017.

As a fully paid-up member of the globalised metropolitan elite, so enthusiastic about openness that I had a refugee to stay for three months and boasted about it in *The Times* … I shall applaud from my bath chair if the nation is populated by rainbow-skinned transsexuals doing Masai dances around our maypoles in 40 years' time.[9]

Ms Duncan's attitudes infuse *The Economist*'s world view and sit very comfortably alongside that of the BBC. Of course, the BBC would never explicitly outline its beliefs in the way Ms Duncan does – to do so would shatter the elaborately constructed pretence that the BBC is neutral on such matters – but can anyone doubt that privately it would take no issue with any of the sentiments she expresses? The Corporation is a strident cheerleader for globalisation, immigration and 'diversity' (a quality which, in BBC usage, is always to be applauded, even though academic studies have shown that too much diversity lessens community cohesion), and when Lord Patten was its boss he clearly found himself in an organisation that he found satisfyingly congenial. Here is another extract from his 2016 speech at the Reuters Institute:

The BBC tells us things we didn't know about the world,

---

9 Emma Duncan, 'Don't assume Brexit attitudes will die out', *The Times*, 3 March 2018.

including things we probably didn't want to know but should. It makes us think, even when thinking is uncomfortable. I am not one of those who denies that the media have an effect on the way society sees itself. How could they not? But I look at modern British society, more comfortable with diversity of opinion, of gender, of race, of religion and lack of it, of sex and sexuality, more comfortable perhaps than any other major nation in the world. I don't know whether that has been merely reflected by the media or influenced by the media – I think probably both – but Britain is a better place for it, and I'm proud that a Conservative Prime Minister is unflinching in his support for the diversity of modern Britain, even though it stands in such contrast to the England of my youth.

Lord Patten's confidence that everything was moving in exactly the direction he approved of – with the BBC leading the way down the path of liberal enlightenment – was about to take a nasty knock. A few weeks after he spoke, the country voted to leave the EU. This came as an unanticipated – and deeply resented – setback for people like him and Emma Duncan who, up to that moment, had experienced only success in making their favoured social agenda a reality.

Lord Patten's belief that Britain is 'a better place' because social mores have moved in a liberal direction is, of course, contentious. It might once upon a time have seemed odd that someone who describes himself as a 'conservative', and a Roman Catholic to boot, should welcome so wholeheartedly the jettisoning of traditional moral attitudes. But the fact that he does tells us much about the climate of opinion within the modern Conservative Party. And the key to understanding how it is that 'conservatives' have failed to defend conservative values over the past fifty years is contained in his observation that the media itself has had an influence on this process. Lord Patten is rather coy about this, positing the idea only as a possibility about which he himself is unsure. He was being far too modest. It is the contention of this book that it is the media in general, and the BBC in particular, that has been the strongest factor in the long battle to vanquish social conservatism in Britain. This has been achieved by first mocking, then marginalising and finally ignoring altogether the concerns of social conservatives. Many debates on the BBC now do not include anyone with a socially conservative viewpoint. In BBC-world we are all liberals now.

At the heart of this story, is a nexus of media interests which is militantly liberal in outlook, and which has systematically destroyed the foundational beliefs and practices which informed the lives of previous generations. This process started in the post-war years, gathered strength in the 1960s and, since then, has enjoyed virtually uninterrupted success in the furtherance of its goals (the EU referendum is the exception and, at the time of writing, it is not clear whether the wishes of the voters will actually result in Britain leaving the EU, such is the ferocity of the fightback against Brexit).

There have been many players in this long game – crusading lawyers, activist judges, organised pressure groups – but the most important by far has been the BBC itself. It has always been ready to put its massive weight behind any campaign which sits within the liberal social agenda. It has not acted alone, but has been encouraged and bolstered by other like-minded media outfits – *The Guardian* and *The Economist* among them. Its centrality in the UK's media landscape has dragged the rest of the broadcasters with it: ITV, Channel 4 and Sky all sing more or less from the same song sheet. Unlike in the US (where Fox network is stridently different from the others) there is, to this day, no national broadcaster in Britain which champions a conservative social agenda. Given the absence of dissenting voices, it is no wonder that from his lofty perch Lord Patten imagined a Britain at ease with itself and united in its love of 'diversity'; he wasn't hearing any dissenting voices because, in mainstream British broadcasting, there aren't any. So completely has the social conservative view been eclipsed in media-land that I suspect many programme-makers do not even understand that there might be a valid view different from their own. It is one of the ironies of the current situation that in the 1960s social liberals considered themselves to be 'counter-cultural'. But they can no longer claim to be so. The only authentic counter-culture in contemporary Britain is social conservatism and, as is always the case, at first a counter-culture has to struggle to get a hearing. That's what the social liberals did in the 1960s: firstly within the BBC, and then throughout wider society, their views prevailed. Once in charge they were able to use the BBC's resources to evangelise for their beliefs, which they have done to great effect. The Britain of the twenty-first century is a country shaped by the BBC as surely as the hands of the potter mould the clay on the wheel.

CHAPTER TWO

THE BBC AND BREXIT

T HERE'S A PHRASE PEOPLE sometimes use about the BBC; they call it the 'national broadcaster'. But no one should imagine that the words can be taken to imply that the BBC acts as some kind of national cheerleader; rather the opposite is in fact true, for the BBC is much more comfortable in the role of chief prosecutor. The mother country is always fair game, while most BBC journalists show a squeamish reluctance to voice any criticisms that might be thought to offend foreign sensibilities. In the BBC's view, the foreigner is usually right, or, at the very least, deserves the benefit of the doubt. The BBC gets mightily affronted by any suggestion that it might, in some circumstances, be expected to demonstrate a measure of patriotic solidarity.

Throughout my twenty-five years working as a BBC reporter I was often struck by the sense of detachment from purely national interests that is central to the ethos of BBC journalism. This is sometimes a very good thing: it inculcates an objectivity which, properly applied, allows the audience to hear both sides of an argument untainted by a patriotic gloss. However, it can have the unwonted side effect of making BBC reports sound rather bloodless, as if broadcast from some distant planet inhabited by journalists who do not share the same interests or emotions as the audience. It can give an unfortunate sense that the BBC is broadcasting *de haut en bas* and, at its worst, can make the BBC sound actively hostile to the foreign policy aims of the government of the day.

There was a telling exchange on *Newsnight* in June of 2017 that illustrates the point. Andrea Leadsom, Leader of the House, was being interviewed about Brexit by Emily Maitlis, who was pouring scorn on the government's negotiating position. At one point Ms Maitlis said, 'They're laughing at us', to which Leadsom replied, 'It would be helpful if broadcasters were willing to be a little bit patriotic. The country took a decision and this government is determined to deliver on that decision.' Ms Maitlis reacted as if she'd been accused of something shameful; 'Are you accusing me of being unpatriotic?' she demanded, stung by the politician's effrontery in suggesting that 'We all need to pull together'. Many people might see the sense in Leadsom's modest plea – after all, the

Brexit negotiations are important, and the agreement that is eventually reached will affect everyone in the country, including BBC employees, for good or ill. But to Corporation journalists the very idea that they should be patriotic (of all quaint notions!) is an intolerable affront. A couple of days after the interview Mark Damazer,[1] controller of BBC Radio 4 from 2004–2010, entered the fray. When I worked in the Corporation and started to complain about what I perceived as its inherent bias I crossed swords with a number of high-level executives, Mark Damazer among them. He is the kind of man who doesn't trouble himself overmuch about trying to conceal the sense of intellectual superiority that he deeply and sincerely feels. After the *Newsnight* exchange Damazer rode to Maitlis's defence. Writing in *The Times*' 'Thunderer' column, he began:

> Andrea Leadsom's call in the *Newsnight* studio on Friday for broadcasters to dig for victory in the Brexit negotiations by asking them to find their echt [German for 'authentic'] patriotism (as she would not put it) is beyond parody. But although my outrage meter, honed by 30 years at the BBC, went straight into the red zone on listening to Leadsom's assertion … the happy truth is that the sheer witlessness

---

1 Mr Damazer is now the Master of St Peter's College, Oxford – one of an increasing number of BBC luminaries who head up Oxbridge colleges. For an account of the author's own disagreements with Damazer, see: *Can We Trust the BBC?* (Continuum, 2007).

of her remarks will ensure they have no impact on news and current affairs journalists at all.[2]

After going on to say, with immense condescension, that Leadsom's remarks should be seen as 'naive and daft rather than intended to be menacing' he delivered the following dictum:

> The BBC's refusal (and not only the BBC's) over decades to allow the 'patriotic interest' to be defined by the government – any government – is what keeps it alive … So Leadsom will just have to put up with the fact that both inside the UK and outside it the BBC's legitimacy and reputation derive from resisting the banal and anti-democratic assumption that once a vote takes place it should go easy and become in effect an arm of the state, or at least a publicly funded cheerleader.[3]

Clearly, it's bad enough to be accused of being unpatriotic – but perhaps the one thing worse for a BBC employee would be to run the risk of being labelled an actual patriot! Exaggeration and caricature are, of course, legitimate tools in any

---

2 Mark Damazer, 'Leadsom was wrong to ask the BBC to be "a bit patriotic"', *The Times*, 26 June 2017.

3 Mark Damazer, ibid.

columnist's armoury, but Mr Damazer's disdain was surely an unbalanced response to Leadsom's suggestion that the BBC might occasionally try thinking of itself as on Britain's side in the Brexit negotiations. That might seem quite a small thing to ask for, but it is certainly not the flavour of the BBC's Brexit coverage to date, which has been typified by a neurotic pessimism where every negative possibility is accentuated, and every bit of good news played down or ignored.

It is certainly right and proper that the BBC should subject government ministers to tough questioning, particularly on an issue as important as Brexit, but it should be unbiased. Indeed, according to its solemn charter promise to be impartial, it must be even-handed. In the Brexit context that means being equally tough on EU politicians and officials when they are interviewed and, so far, that is something the BBC has conspicuously failed to be. It has become increasingly clear as the Brexit negotiations have progressed, that it is the EU, not Britain, which has been the main obstacle to progress. The EU Commission (and it is important to make a distinction between that body and member governments) is plainly bent on obstructing a mutually beneficial free trade agreement as a way of punishing the UK. For the hard-working people of Europe, spread across the twenty-eight member countries this is tantamount to economic self-harm, inflicted by the very people in Brussels charged with looking after their interests. BBC journalists could demonstrate their own *echt* patriotism in the Brexit context merely by holding the EU to account in the same way as they do the British government. But there is no appetite for this within the BBC – even when it is quite clear that the EU is being obtuse. Time and again EU apologists are listened to respectfully, their assertions taken as reasonable and true, their truculent objections to British proposals given reverential weight. The sharp-edged, attack-dog treatment is reserved solely for British ministers. Why should this be?

The answer requires an understanding of the BBC's deep, sincere and abiding love affair with the EU. The roots of this affair lie in the Corporation's instinctive internationalism, and go back right to the foundation of the organisation. The visitor to Broadcasting House in Portland Place is greeted with the BBC's motto inlaid in the floor: 'Nation shall speak peace unto nation' it reads. It is thought the inspiration for the wording comes from a Biblical source: the Book of Micah 4:3, which reads: 'Nation shall not lift up a sword against nation, neither shall they learn war any more'. The wording of the motto is as old as the BBC itself, dating back to the organisation's inception on 1 January 1927 and they express a noble sentiment which doubtless had an especial resonance in a country where the awful wounds of the Great War were still raw. And the BBC strove hard to live up to this high-minded sentiment. Indeed, the next couple of decades were those in which the BBC first established the reputation for truth telling that provided it with a store of moral capital ever since.

The war years of 1939–45 were a time of BBC greatness. In her vastly overrated novel *Human Voices*, which focuses on the wartime BBC, Penelope Fitzgerald claims that the Corporation was 'dedicated to the strangest project of the war, or of any war, that is telling the truth.' In this, the writer was perhaps stretching the truth a little herself: during the war years the BBC did not always tell the whole truth – how could it? There were lives at risk – but it did its best, within the limits imposed by military censors. Edward Stourton, a BBC man for thirty years, makes the point in his book *Auntie's War: The BBC during the Second World War*[4] that throughout those years a 'golden thread of truth' ran through the broadcasts. But, even so, there were times when the BBC put a heavy gloss on events – the mythologising of the evacuation at Dunkirk is one of the best-known examples. You can still find the reports from those dramatic days on the BBC website. Even today they bring a lump to the throat; the reporters stress the cheerfulness of the soldiers and the heroism of sailors who rescued them. But it was the novelist and social commentator J. B. Priestley who captured the mood best of all. In a 'Postcript' broadcast a few days after the evacuation he spoke of an 'English epic' where the 'funny little steamers' set sail on an 'excursion to hell' and returned 'brave and battered' with the remnants of the British

---

4   Edward Stourton, *Auntie's War: The BBC during the Second World War* (Doubleday, 2016).

Expeditionary Force. And it is his version of Dunkirk that has passed into folk-legend. How the 'small ships' saved the day. What you will not find from the BBC broadcasts of those days is any clear exposition of the scale of the disaster which had befallen the British Army.

Dunkirk was the moment of maximum peril for the country and the BBC, in the interests of national morale, rightly chose to disguise the extent of the military failure which, in truth, the evacuation had been. It should also be remembered that George Orwell, who worked at the BBC during the war in charge of broadcasts to India, based (in part at least) his sinister 'Ministry of Truth' in *Nineteen Eighty-Four* on his experiences at the BBC. It is said he got the idea for the regime's newspeak from his exposure to the language of internal BBC memorandums. But, these caveats aside, even the harshest critic would be forced to concede that the wartime Corporation acquitted itself with honour. And there could be no question about the Corporation's essential patriotism. But what came next?

In the 1950s the BBC acquired a reputation for unbearable stuffiness. Perhaps it was a hangover from the war years, but the language of every broadcast was subject to strict monitoring where every phrase was scrutinised for any hint of impropriety; so naturally, creative types trying to script comedy shows or dramas chafed under the strictures. Bawdiness, vulgarity and the erotic have always been essential ingredients in drama and literature and the BBC's puritanism could not withstand the pressure. By the 1960s change was in the air; a younger generation at the BBC, not formed by wartime experiences, began to push the boundaries. It was during these years that the BBC began to embrace satire as an irreverent intake to poke fun at their strait-laced elders. The older generation resisted, but their opposition proved futile; it was the spirit of the age they were fighting, and the BBC began to embrace a sharper, edgier type of programme. Meanwhile, out in the real world, Britain was beset with problems: there was the trauma of dismantling the Empire, for so long a cause of pride, and the country's economic performance was weak compared to its continental competitors. These were the years of Germany's Wirtschaftswunder, France's *trente glorieuses* and Italy's *miracolo economico* – in other words, those decades when from among the ruins of their devastated societies the European nations enjoyed a prolonged spurt of economic growth, which laid the foundations of today's prosperity.

Among Britain's political class in the '60s and '70s, this European economic renaissance only added to the mood of defeatism that gripped politicians, diplomats, academics and journalists alike. Collectively, and wistfully, they looked across the Channel to countries enjoying a seemingly inexorable economic rise. In Britain, by comparison, the economy was struggling – industrial relations were catastrophically bad and national prosperity seemed a distant prospect. This mood persisted, perhaps worsened, even after accession to the EEC in 1973. The pessimistic mood was captured perfectly by Sir Nicholas Henderson, who had been our man in Bonn and Paris. In 1979, just before Mrs Thatcher won the general election, he wrote his valedictory dispatch to then Foreign Secretary David Owen. This extract gives a flavour of the despair gripping the country's ruling class:

> Our decline in relation to our European partners has been so marked that today we are not only no longer a world power, but we are not in the first rank even as a European one. Income per head in Britain is now, for the first time for over 300 years, below that in France. We are scarcely in the same economic league as the Germans or French. We talk of ourselves without shame as being one of the less prosperous countries of Europe. The prognosis for the foreseeable future is discouraging. If present trends continue we shall be overtaken in GDP per head by Italy and Spain well before the end of the century.

As is clear from this the country's ruling class was in a complete funk and had quite lost its nerve. It was in this atmosphere of despair that the BBC's attitude to the European project was fashioned. We had joined what was then, allegedly, a purely economic project, just at the moment of maximum national weakness. The talk was all of 'managing decline', with many of the country's most prominent voices predicting an irreversible descent into the second rank of nations. What happened next demonstrated the inherent unpredictability of human affairs and the fate of nations. Mrs Thatcher explicitly rejected the notion of 'managed decline' and set about tackling long-standing problems with reformist zeal. In the following decades Britain experienced its own version of those *trente glorieuses*, and all those gloomy predictions proved to be a collective bad dream. But within the BBC there was a stout, almost fanatical adherence to the doctrine of national decline, and a corresponding resistance to Thatcher and all her works. As a London-based BBC reporter in those years I saw first-hand how deeply the BBC establishment opposed what came to be known as 'Thatcherism'. Not least among her crimes, in their eyes, was her combative and oppositional stance towards the EU. They hated the fact that she failed to display the appropriate level of humility in her dealings with Brussels that our supposed decline merited.

It was in the 1980s that the battle lines on the European issue first came to be delineated. The first use of the term 'Euroscepticism' was in *The Times* on 11 November 1985 and it came to denote opposition to, and suspicion of moves towards, greater European integration. The small band of sceptics, including people like Richard Body MP and John Redwood MP, were viewed by the BBC as unenlightened jingoists, of little account in the wider scheme of things, and were much mocked.

When Argentina invaded the Falkland Islands in 1982, and Mrs Thatcher sent a naval task force to recover them, the BBC (for a while, at least) mislaid entirely its patriotism – so outraged was opinion within Broadcasting House by her anachronistic martial spirit (any vote on the matter within the BBC would undoubtedly have handed the islands over to General Galtieri without further ado). A memo was sent out to BBC news editors making it plain that the BBC should avoid any sense of partiality when talking about the conflict:

NOT OUR TROOPS: we should try to avoid using 'our' when we mean British. We are not Britain. We are the BBC.

Things came to something of a climax when BBC news bulletins began to give statements from the military junta in Buenos Aires the same standing as those from our own government. BBC newsreaders began to say things like, 'The government in London claims...', as if the BBC had completely psychologically detached itself from the nation. We were a long way from the Dunkirk spirit. Protests followed and the Corporation backed down, realising perhaps that its own detachment hit a false note when it was British servicemen who were risking their lives out there in the South Atlantic.

But, Falklands episode aside, history, it seemed, was on the side of the pro-European establishment, and it was a sweet moment of triumph for the BBC when, in 1990, Mrs Thatcher was toppled – her downfall, in large measure, the consequence of her innate Euroscepticism. Her replacement, John Major, the protégé and close ally of the fanatical Europhile Michael Heseltine, was a man of very different stripe. Major proved himself dedicated to the cause of ever closer European integration despite the unremitting opposition of a minority of his own MPs. The bloody political battles of the Major years scarred the Tory Party and led to the difficult-to-refute (though completely untrue) charge that the divisions over Europe were purely a matter of internal party politics of little interest to the wider public. It was only the 2016 referendum result on EU membership that showed that the sceptics actually spoke for a majority of the population.

From the early days of Euroscepticism onward the critics were well aware that the BBC was firmly in the other camp. BBC coverage of the European issue framed it almost exclusively in economic terms; it was all about how impossible it would be for Britain to prosper outside the EU, and there was little interest in what has always been the most important, principled, objection to membership. Namely, the democratic deficit which it naturally entails. The European Union is a novelty in world affairs – a supranational body to which free-standing democratic nations have ceded sovereign power. It is something more than a confederation of independent states, but something significantly less than a unified federation like the United States. But the direction of travel within Europe towards the creation of a federated superstate has been unmistakeable, and it was the lack of full consent from the British people that was always the foundation of the sceptics' opposition. It is undeniably true that when Britain joined what was then called the European Economic Community in 1973, there was no public understanding of, nor consent given for, a move towards dissolving the British state within a European entity, although in retrospect this seems implicit.

The founding fathers of the European Union recognised, from the beginning, that supranationalism was to be the cornerstone of the new system, as is clear from the declaration made on 18 April 1951, the day the same founding fathers signed the Treaty of Paris:

> By the signature of this Treaty, the participating Parties give proof of their determination to create the first supranational institution and that thus they are laying the true foundation of an organised Europe. This Europe remains open to all nations. We profoundly hope that other nations will join us in our common endeavour.

The BBC's clear duty should have been to air the subject of what supranationalism meant, fully, openly and exhaustively, particularly as the sceptic movement grew in strength. The implications of the phrase 'organised Europe' should have been minutely dissected to understand its consequences, but the BBC shirked that duty. And here is the essence of the noble lie as it pertains to the EU and the BBC: because it wished to preserve Britain's membership of the EU, sincerely believing it to be in the country's best interests, the Corporation relegated that critical debate to one of secondary importance while, at the same time, elevating the economic debate to pre-eminence. This was deeply frustrating to sceptics who struggled to get the BBC to engage with what to them was the very heart of their case – for there can be no more important subject, within a democracy, than the actual location of power: was it Westminster, or was it to be Brussels? And if it was to be Brussels, how could the ordinary voter make their concerns known to a distant – and foreign – group of rulers?

There was a further consequence of the muffling of the debate about democracy; an inchoate cynicism grew about the real intentions of our political establishment. There was a growing feeling that the country was not being told the truth about the destination our leaders were planning for us; that they had privately predetermined the outcome which was to be that of a European superstate – a notion, however, that was routinely dismissed as a figment of fevered Eurosceptic imaginings. In hindsight, and with the result of the membership referendum known to us, we can see that that suspicion fed the public mood which resulted in the vote to leave. There was an essential dishonesty about the pro-European project stemming right from its earliest days; the pretence was that there were no important democratic consequences of membership.

There is nothing inherently wrong in the idea of a supranational federation of European states – in many ways it might be seen to be a noble, even desirable, project – but what seems clearly wrong is to inveigle a free country into such a federation under false pretences. The European Union is very much a work in progress, but there is now no disguising what its masters see as the desired destination; it is possible that the British people could have been persuaded to sign up, but that would have required a quite different approach from the country's leaders. They would have had to make the case for positive engagement, fully recognising that joining would mean the gradual, but remorseless, loss of national sovereignty to the point – somewhere in the future – where the idea of 'Britain' as a national entity ceased altogether, having been subsumed by a greater European state. How different things might have turned out had the debate been conducted as it should have been – with honesty and candour – we shall now never know, because the BBC failed to force the crucial argument into the open.

There were constant complaints about the BBC's alleged pro-European bias from the sceptics throughout the 1990s. The BBC, of course, is often buffeted by claims of bias from the protagonists in any hotly debated topic, but the Eurosceptics had good grounds for suspicion. There is, for instance, the intriguing, and still shocking, case of Jack de Manio, the star presenter of the *Today* programme back in the early '70s when Britain was making its bid to join the EEC. A discreet propaganda unit at the Foreign Office, the Information Research Department, worked behind the scenes cultivating important journalists to bring them onside with the government's position. One of the IRD's key people was a PR man, Geoffrey Tucker, a talented networker and passionate pro-European. In 2000, Tucker revealed that de Manio had been identified as an obstacle: he was seen as far too hostile to the whole European project. Tucker said:

> Jack de Manio was a presenter who was terribly anti-European and we protested privately about this and he was moved. Whether that was coincidence or not I really don't know. I'm sure a lot of people would say that undue pressure was not applied, but I don't think the spin doctors would find that strange at all today. I just said listening to him it seems this man is giving a totally unbalanced view. It would appear that there is nothing good about Europe at all. And Ian Trethowan listened and Jack de Manio was replaced.[5]

---

5   Geoffrey Tucker was interviewed for the Radio 4 programme *Document* in an edition called 'Letters to The Times' in February 2000. The producer of this programme encountered stiff internal resistance to broadcasting what she had uncovered about the de Manio story. But, in the end, the programme was allowed to go out.

This story is a good illustration of how the establishment works and how it exerts controls on the BBC – and things have not changed. In 2017 there were rumours that the BBC was under pressure from important Remainers to rein in John Humphrys – the senior presenter on *Today*. He was seen as being too much of a sceptic about the EU; happily – perhaps afraid of the likely reaction to such a move – Mr Humphrys remains in post – and is still one of the most feared of BBC interrogators. The de Manio story was not known to the Eurosceptics of the 1990s as they battled to get a fair hearing; they only had the evidence of their own ears – the pro-European tone of the BBC's coverage, the ignoring of their concerns about democratic accountability and the denigration of their cause. Many complaints were made, but the BBC is well-practised in the art of stonewalling those who feel the Corporation has done them down. But the intervention of two rich individuals were about to redress the balance somewhat.

The first was Sir James Goldsmith, an Anglo-French multi-millionaire, who had become increasingly concerned about the growing German domination of Europe. His fears crystallised around the 1993 decision to change the name of the European Economic Community to the European Union. Goldsmith was elected to the European Parliament in 1994 under the banner of the Movement for France – a Eurosceptic outfit – but in 1994 he switched his focus to British politics and announced the formation of the Referendum Party. The party had a single purpose – to campaign for the British people to have a vote on further European integration. It proposed to put the following question to a plebiscite:

> Do you want the United Kingdom to be part of a federal Europe or do you want the United Kingdom to return to an association of sovereign nations that are part of a common trading market?

Goldsmith had enjoyed close relations with the Tory Party under Mrs Thatcher, but he viewed John Major's administration as betraying her legacy – particularly on the European issue. The attitude of the political establishment towards Goldsmith was disdainful: Douglas Hurd, a pro-European Tory grandee – spoke disparagingly of 'millionaires who play with British politics as a hobby', but for all the efforts to dismiss him there is circumstantial evidence, at least, that he put the wind up the Tories. In 1996, a year before the expected date of the general election, the Conservatives pledged themselves to hold a referendum before entering into 'economic and monetary union' (EMU) – shorthand for what was expected to be the next great leap forward in building the European project. The Labour Party followed suit, nervous of being outflanked on an issue where it was clear that many voters had misgivings about the direction of travel.

Goldsmith refused to be deflected by the Tories' repositioning on the issue and went ahead with his campaign, spending millions on advertising in the run-up to the 1997 general election. His party fielded 547 candidates and, because of that, the BBC grudgingly allowed him one party political broadcast (they refused him the three he said he was entitled to by virtue of his party's number of candidates). He used his one opportunity to lambast the Corporation, labelling it 'the Brussels News Corporation'. In the event, the Referendum Party polled 811,827 votes, just 2.6 per cent of the total, and many mainstream commentators wrote off the whole Referendum Party's intervention as an irrelevant failure. Psephologists said that the votes he siphoned off had cost the Tories about sixteen seats, which seemed almost irrelevant on the night, when Tony Blair's landslide delivered him a parliamentary majority of 179. But that dry statistical analysis rather misses the point.

In retrospect his intervention from 1994 onwards can be seen as critical; arguably it altered the course of British history. Without him, Labour, which won a landslide in the 1997 election, would not have been lumbered with its promise to hold a referendum on EMU. Tony Blair was very much in favour of Britain participating in EMU, but baulked at the prospect of honouring that promise, fearing that a loss would drain away precious political capital early in his first administration. Sir James Goldsmith died a few weeks after the 1997 election, but his legacy was the agreement of all the major parties that the British people should be consulted before any further European integration; it was another nineteen years before David Cameron had to make good on the promise, but the fact that he did owes much to Goldsmith.

Throughout the 1990s the BBC did not unduly trouble itself over the complaints from Eurosceptics about bias. Although the Corporation has a formal complaints procedure, very few complainants get much in the way of satisfaction from it; anyone who does embark upon a complaint against the BBC will find themselves in a protracted exercise which rarely delivers satisfaction. The BBC is loath, in the extreme, to make on-air corrections or apologies and defends its prerogatives with vigour. One of the problems with allegations of bias is the difficulty of proving them – 'bias' is a very subjective thing. But one man proved that with determination, and by spending a lot of money, it was possible to amass convincing evidence; he was Lord Pearson of Rannoch. A Eurosceptic of longstanding in the 1990s, Rannoch became increasingly frustrated by what he saw as the BBC's obvious bias. He decided to bankroll a detailed analysis of BBC output. The methodology was simple, if laborious; his researchers listened and watched thousands of hours of BBC news and current affairs output over a five-year period. This massive undertaking resulted in a series of complaints to the BBC – all backed up with statistical data. On the basis of the figures, the researchers concluded that there was a long-standing bias towards pro-European speakers of about 2:1. In addition, they found an overemphasis on Tory Party divisions and a massive under-representation of Labour Eurosceptics as well as erroneous, pro-EU reportage. Faced with this body of evidence the BBC finally, in the autumn of 2004, set up an inquiry into its own coverage.

The panel charged with this task comprised two known Europhiles and two sceptics under the chairmanship of a distinguished academic, Lord Wilson of Dinton, Master of Emmanuel College, Cambridge. The resulting Wilson Report, published in January 2005, largely vindicated the sceptics' complaints, although in an attempt to save face for the BBC, it found there had been no 'conscious or deliberate bias'. But, notwithstanding that caveat, the panel concluded: 'although the BBC wishes to be impartial in its news coverage of the EU it is not succeeding.' Lord Pearson had won his battle and the BBC was put on notice that it had to clean up its act.

There were signs that the BBC began, from that point onwards, to police its own output on the EU a little more scrupulously. From my own private sources, I know that individual correspondents were instructed that they had to make more of an effort to fairly represent the Eurosceptic case; it didn't stop all the grumbles, many sceptics still perceived an underlying bias against them, but it's fair to say that from 2005 onwards there was a greater awareness within the BBC of the need to strike the right balance – even if the facts show a spectacular imbalance in the coverage continued unabated. One of the most striking findings in Lord Pearson's research was that in the years between 2005 and 2015, of the 4,275 guests invited on to talk about the EU, only 132 – amounting to 3.2 per cent – supported the UK leaving the EU.[6]

The big test came with the referendum campaign of 2015/16; with the UK's membership of the EU now on the line, would the BBC prove itself to be fair-minded, impartial and balanced? There were many sceptics who feared the worst.

But in the event, the BBC proved them quite wrong. In a reversal of the usual pattern, after the result was known, it was the Europhiles, not the usual suspects, who were furious. In his fascinating book, the *Sunday Times*' political editor Tim Shipman gives a blow-by-blow account of the EU referendum. He quotes an unnamed member of the Britain Stronger in Europe board as having said:

> I say this with great trepidation because I love the BBC and I hate people who criticise the BBC, but unfortunately the BBC was terrible for us. They got obsessed about having to have equal billing on every side of the argument. You'd have the IMF, then you'd have a crackpot economist, or you'd have an FTSE 100 CEO and then someone who makes a couple of prams in Sheffield. It was balanced in terms of

---

6   Tim Shipman, *All Out War: The Full Story of How Brexit Sank Britain's Political Class* (William Collins, 2016).

the amount of coverage, but not balanced in terms of the quality of the people.[7]

What is striking about this quote – aside from its pungent snobbery – is the way in which this individual was quite unable to see the exquisite irony of their complaint. For years the Europhiles had been able to rely on a supportive BBC to bolster their position and marginalise the sceptics, but when it came to the referendum campaign the rules changed. The BBC was not only honour-bound to give equal coverage to both sides, but it was legally obliged to do so under the Representation of the People Act. That is the law which governs broadcasting during elections and referendums. In the so-called 'short campaign' – the final four weeks up to polling day itself – when the majority of the public properly engaged with the debate, the BBC had no leeway: it had to be 50/50 between Leave and Remain.

The main complaint of the Remain side was that the Leavers got away with telling lies that the BBC did not call out. It will be up to the individual reader for themselves to decide whether the Remain campaign itself was always scrupulously truthful, but regardless, the complaint betrays a misunderstanding of where the BBC's duty lay. The Corporation could not have been party to a process which 'fact-checked' the arguments of only one side – that would have been to invite bitter complaints

7   Tim Shipman, ibid.

about an obvious unfairness, particularly as the Leavers were in a state of high alert for any signs of bias against them. And, in point of fact, the claims of both Leavers and Remainers were based on assumptions, guesswork and predictions: for instance, the stories frequently told by the Remain campaign foretelling economic ruin if Britain voted to leave – the so-called 'Project Fear' masterminded by George Osborne. In reality neither side's claims occupied territory where 'truth' could ever be established, because both were in the game of predicting an unknown future.

There was another factor in the campaign: the skill with which the two sides played the media. Shipman's conclusion is that in the heat of battle it was the Leave campaign, under the control of Dominic Cummings, which played the smarter game. Shipman's view is that Cummings was lighter on his feet and understood how to get the coverage he wanted. He was the better media street fighter. Remain, by comparison, often seemed flat-footed. Leave concentrated on a few, easily understood messages and stuck to them throughout, and the BBC's obligation to a 50/50 split meant that Leave's core message was endlessly repeated. There's a term for that – 'media amplification' – and it's what those in marketing have always understood: if you want to get the message through, endless repetition is the key. Clever tactics helped win the day.

And then... It was all over. In post-war Britain there has never been the equal of the political shockwave that came after the vote on Thursday 23 June 2016. Politics is an arena prone to inflated language, where all adjectives are debased verbal currency, but it can be said, without exaggeration, that the vote to leave the EU was the biggest upset in modern political history. It upturned almost every commentator's prediction and it left the British establishment in the wholly novel position of having to deliver a policy with which it profoundly, and sincerely, disagreed. For, when you survey the forces lined up against each other, there was, it seemed, no contest: on the Remain side there was the government, the leadership of all the other main parties, most of the big political figures of previous eras, heavyweight economics outfits like the IMF and OECD alongside most of the heaviest guns from industry and the economics profession (to say nothing of important individuals in churches and civil society). On the other side: a somewhat motley collection of political insurgents backed by some Eurosceptic newspapers and a good sprinkling of mavericks from industry and the professions. And where was the BBC in all this? As just described, during the most intense part of the campaign the BBC delivered exactly what it was obliged to do – even-handed coverage of the issue. But what did they do next?

Nine months after the referendum, in March 2017, seventy-two MPs, from all parties, wrote an open letter accusing the BBC of 'pessimistic and skewed' coverage of the Brexit issue. The letter was organised by Tory MP Julian Knight, a former

BBC journalist himself, and someone who actually backed Remain. What had so thoroughly riled the MPs was the mood of neurotic pessimism – bordering on despair – which coloured all the Corporation's coverage of the post-referendum scene. It wasn't only the way in which gloomy predictions from the likes of the CBI, the OECD or any number of pro-Remain economic outfits was always assured top billing, it was also the manner in which any good economic news – of which there was plenty – was prefaced by a Brexit health warning. It became a sort of joke among the sceptics; they called it the I-SOB formula – 'In Spite of Brexit'. So unemployment went on falling 'I-SOB', and inward investment kept on coming, 'I-SOB', etc.

Through the ensuing months and up to the time of writing there has been no change in the BBC's tone; on Brexit it remains lugubrious, downbeat and depressing. Perhaps that's not surprising coming from an organisation which, root and branch, opposes the idea of Britain tearing itself free of Brussels, but such coverage is not without consequences. It emboldens those in the establishment – and there are many – who would like to stop Brexit in its tracks, and it makes clear to the EU itself that Britain is far from united on the issue. It can be argued that the pessimism might even be making it more difficult for Britain to strike a good trade deal; the EU's negotiators listen to the BBC, too, making it a simple matter to work out which buttons to press to generate the most negative coverage. One could argue that with this momentous negotiation entering its critical phase, the BBC should be able to locate its *echt* patriotism. But in this, as in so many other areas, the BBC's preferred stance is one of lofty detachment from the concerns and attitudes of the majority of ordinary people in the country.

CHAPTER THREE

WHAT'S GOING DOWN AT MERITOCRACY CENTRAL?

I N THE AFTERMATH OF the Brexit vote, after the political and social elites had recovered their equilibrium somewhat, came The Great Explanations. These assumed many forms; there were *Guardian* articles which blamed the outcome on the sheer mendacity of the Leave campaign; it was 'lies, all lies'; there were explanations which alleged that Leave voters were all basically just racists and there were those who argued that the Leave vote was just an anti-government spasm, merely aimed at giving David Cameron's regime a kicking. Few commentators understood the real reason; and, as subsequent polling showed, the single most important factor in the minds of Leave voters was the desire to restore proper accountability to government by regaining the power to make our own laws. *The Economist*, in particular, was completely nonplussed by the decision to quit; in the long run-up to the referendum the newspaper (it is one of its idiosyncrasies to so style itself, though to most people it is, in normal usage, rather obviously, a magazine) published a number of reassuring articles about the forthcoming Brexit referendum. Here's a fairly typical quote which appeared 15 October 2015:

> One thing most referendums have in common is that they tend to deliver victories for the status quo. In an EU referendum, says Peter Kellner, the boss of YouGov, a pollster, perhaps 25–30 per cent of the voters may feel strongly that they want to leave and 20–25 per cent may feel equally strongly that they want to stay. After excluding non-voters, that leaves 35–40 per cent who will be undecided. This middle group is more likely to shift towards staying in because they will feel more comfortable with the devil they know.

The hallmark of *The Economist* is its unshakeable confidence in its own judgement (an attribute that has survived, remarkably intact, events like the 2008 global economic crisis which, rather embarrassingly for a magazine that is, after all, devoted to economics, it utterly failed to foresee). After the Brexit vote it proceeded to position itself as among the most pessimistic of all commentators on the consequences, and did so with its usual air of adamantine certainty. This naturally recommended it to the BBC and in the months following the referendum *The Economist*'s editor in chief, Zanny Minton Beddoes, became one of the go-to pundits for the heavyweight current affairs shows. Needless to say, Ms Minton Beddoes forecast calamity and counselled despair.

In all the analysis that subsequently poured out, one stark fact emerged; that the best predictor of how an individual voted was their level of educational attainment. Put crudely, the better educated you were, the more likely it was that you voted to Remain. The correlation between the two things is, in a statistical sense, compelling. In February 2017 the BBC website published a detailed breakdown of voting using the results from more than half the voting wards in the country which confirmed the link beyond argument. For example in Cambridge, certainly among the best educated places in the world, the Remain vote came in at 73.8 per cent, while in Oxford it was 70 per cent. But these facts caused difficulties in the ensuing political discourse; no one wanted to draw the obvious (if crass) conclusion – that smart people voted to stay while only dummies opted for Leave. Insulting the voters never was a clever tactic for politicians. Nevertheless, the fact that the better-educated voted to stay in the EU seems irrefutable and demands an explanation that goes beyond labelling Leavers as stupid, racist brutes who don't know where their own best interests lie.

The soul searching that began in the summer of 2016 and continues unabated to this day, eventually began to yield some more sophisticated analysis as to why things had turned out as they did. In particular, some thoughtful commentators were drawn to re-examine a work of fiction by one of the towering figures of the post-war Labour Party, Michael Young. Here's what Adrian Wooldridge – the current occupant of the Bagehot column in *The Economist* which pronounces on British politics – wrote in February 2018:

> After much searching, Bagehot has found a book that at last explains what is going on in British politics. This wonderful volume not only reveals the deeper reasons for all the bizarre convulsions. It also explains why things are not likely to get better any time soon. The book is Michael Young's 'The Rise of the Meritocracy' – and it was published 60 years ago this year.

The reason for Mr Wooldridge's excitement is that *The Rise of the Meritocracy*, a novel, envisions a revolt in Britain in 2033, by the less educated and successful against their rulers – the 'meritocrats' (a word that Michael Young invented). Young's thesis was that in modern Britain it is educational attainment, not accident of birth, which determines worldly success. The meritocracy has supplanted the aristocracy. And while this might seem at first glance to be an overwhelmingly positive development (it is, after all, difficult to make a good argument for the less well-educated being in charge), Young presciently forecasts the problems that would arise; on the one hand the winners, the meritocrats, would be tempted to an insufferable self-satisfaction because they could claim their success was all their own doing; on the other hand, the losers, who had failed to apply themselves and pass their exams, would have no one to blame but themselves. Inevitably, Young conjectured, the losers would become embittered and, finally, would use their voting muscle to overturn the rule of the meritocracy.

One can see why Bagehot felt he had stumbled on the key to understanding Brexit – a vote he deplores as an act of economic self-harm. The parallels are striking, are they not? And they fit very neatly with the statistical analysis of who voted for which side.

There is a huge irony about Michael Young's work, and it is that he wrote the book as a warning; a 'meritocracy' in his view was not a good thing at all and yet, from more or less the time the word was coined, it was co-opted by others, particularly politicians, as an aspirational word. It was what they wanted the country to become and they spoke in glowing terms about a 'meritocratic Britain'. Michael Young tried hard to get people to use the word in the way he originally intended, but it had escaped into the wider world beyond the control of its creator. In a *Guardian* article in June 2001 he criticised Prime Minister Tony Blair for his heedless use of the term:

I have been sadly disappointed by my 1958 book, *The Rise of the Meritocracy*. I coined a word which has gone into general circulation, especially in the United States, and most recently found a prominent place in the speeches of Mr Blair. The book was a satire meant to be a warning (which needless to say has not been heeded) against what might happen in Britain between 1958 and the imagined final revolt against the meritocracy in 2033.

Much that was predicted has already come about. It is highly unlikely the prime minister has read the book, but he has caught on to the word without realising the dangers of what he is advocating.

Young (who died a few months after the article was printed) went on to spell out the problems he saw arising. While it makes good sense, he said, for people to be appointed to do jobs on merit, the danger arises when those same people harden into a new social class to which entry is restricted. In that system, those judged to have no merit would be excluded and, in his words, 'No underclass has ever been left as morally naked as that.'

The article was written at a moment of maximum national hubris; it was just days after Blair's second landslide election and a few weeks before the attack on the Twin Towers on 9/11. A moment when Blair's Britain seemed a land of milk and honey and, for those 'meritocrats' who saw Blair as one of their own, nothing clouded the horizon. And Michael Young did not much care for the new ruling class:

> They can be insufferably smug, much more so than the people who knew they had achieved advancement not on their own merit but because they were, as somebody's son or daughter, the beneficiaries of nepotism. The newcomers can actually believe they have morality on their side. So assured have the elite become that there is almost no block on the rewards they arrogate to themselves.

The meritocratic ethos, which Young described and deplored, has penetrated, effortlessly, into every nook and cranny of British society; it is now ingrained and accepted that educational attainment is the *sine qua non* of advancement. Every profession now embraces the meritocratic ethos – and perhaps none more so than the media. A generation ago, in the years when I first worked as a trainee reporter on a local newspaper in the Black Country, a glittering educational CV was an optional extra; I myself was a university drop-out – and few of my then peers had even got that far. Today, entry to the media is fiercely competitive, and many young journalists start out with postgraduate degrees. Nowhere is that phenomenon more obvious than within the BBC. I doubt, very much, there are now any entry-grade people on the editorial side at the BBC who have no degree; why would there be when so many high-fliers queue up to work for the Corporation? It would be a strange selection board that opted for a candidate with only A levels. The BBC, in microcosm, is the living embodiment of Michael Young's dystopian vision.

In fact, the reality of meritocratic Britain is actually worse than anything Young imagined. When he wrote *The Rise of the Meritocracy* he did not know what we now know about IQ, nor anything about what has come to be known as 'assortative mating'. Back in the 1950s some might have had an inkling that IQ was, to some degree, inherited; though the idea is fiercely resisted by some (particularly on the left), an evidence-based approach leads, ineluctably, to the conclusion that to a significant degree your IQ is dependent on your parentage. This theory – which at one level seems self-evident and common-sensical – became the stuff of controversy with the 1994 publication *The Bell Curve, Intelligence and Class Structure in American Life*, by Richard Herrnstein and Charles Murray. Few books have stirred such long-lasting intellectual debate; to this day Charles Murray is greeted by violent protests if he tries to speak on American university campuses. The eponymous bell curve takes its name from the shape of the graph that emerges if you plot the distribution of intelligence across the population. At one end there is a 5 per cent minority with a very low IQ, while at the other end there is 5 per cent with IQ above 125; between the two extremes is the huge bulk of the population – leading to a bell-shaped distribution.

Herrnstein and Murray are considered proper scientific researchers; and although there have been many attempts to discredit their work, their basic conclusions have stood the test of time. But the soundness of their work has done nothing to shield them from attack, and in particular, from the charge of racism. This arose because their research seems to indicate that there is a racial component to variations in intelligence; their findings were that Asian-Americans outscore white Americans who, in turn, outscore African-Americans. The differences were not huge, but they were measurable and consistent. Herrnstein and Murray concluded that intelligence was partly affected by environmental factors, but that a major influence on an individual's IQ was always genetic. They went on to draw some controversial inferences about US social policy on the basis of their findings; for instance, they said that welfare policies encouraged young women of low IQ to have babies (because the state would support them in single motherhood) whereas more intelligent women, who tend to have fewer babies, received no such encouragement from the state in older age.

In retrospect, it is completely unsurprising that the book was controversial; given the combustible nature of racial politics in the US it was inevitable. The claim that intelligence is mainly inherited causes fury on the left and many deny its validity, although the body of research into the subject, which grows by the year, is making that stance increasingly hard to maintain. Take, for instance, the work of the distinguished psycho-geneticist Robert Plomin at the Institute of Psychiatry at Kings College London. In 1994 Professor Plomin (an American by birth) initiated the Twins Early Development Study (TEDS), which follows the development of every set of twins born in Britain between 1994 and 1996. At each stage of their schooling – SATs, GCSEs, A levels etc. – the performance of these twins has been recorded. By using other metrics concerning the performance of identical compared with non-identical and the performance of twins who have been adopted, Professor Plomin has arrived at a firm conclusion: genetics is, by far, the biggest single determinant of academic achievement. In the 'nature versus nurture' argument, he reckons nature (i.e. the individual's genetic make-up) accounts for 50 per cent while nurture (the input from family, schooling and the culture generally) accounts for no more than 20 per cent. He presents this as a value-neutral, evidence-based research finding, but many in education will not accept it as such; on the contrary, they view it as a piece of right-wing dogma.

There is something odd about this reaction. There is a general presumption that all government policy should be 'evidence-based', and yet when evidence is presented which displeases the liberal-left, what ensues can only be described as a tantrum. Here, for instance, is how *The Guardian*, in a 2014 article by Peter Wilby about Professor Plomin's work, begins:

To talk about genes and their links to IQ and educational achievement is to risk accusations of elitism, fascism and racism. When the American professor Arthur Jensen published a paper in 1969 concluding that 80% of variance in IQ scores was attributable to genes, not environment – and attempts to boost African-American scores through pre-school intervention were therefore bound to fail – angry students besieged his office in California. The renowned psychologist Hans Eysenck, who backed Jensen, was punched on the nose while lecturing at the London School of Economics.[1]

The article discusses how a leaked policy paper written by Dominic Cummings for the then education secretary, Michael Gove, had claimed that genetic inheritance was by far the most important determinant of GCSE results. By comparison, schools, teachers and neighbourhoods were, Cummings claimed, comparatively unimportant. Wilby goes on to say that 'teachers have always been suspicious of supporters of nature against nurture because they seem to imply that a child's fate is predetermined and anything schools do is pointless'.

The alarm that Professor Plomin's works engenders in some was amusingly on display when he was invited on to the BBC

---

1   Peter Wilby, 'Psychologist on a mission to give every child a Learning Chip', *The Guardian*, 18 February 2014.

Radio 4 programme *The Life Scientific* in October 2015. Anyone who has listened to this programme knows its style to be comfortable and non-confrontational. It is designed as a vehicle to allow distinguished scientists to describe their careers and explain their work and the interviewer, Jim Al-Khalili, has a gentle style which often coaxes fascinating insights out of his subjects. His interview with Professor Plomin, by contrast, was unusually challenging. Al-Khalili usually takes what his guests have to say at face value – they, after all, are acknowledged experts in their field – but he couldn't resist challenging Plomin. He began one question, 'My concern would be…', then proceeded to air the view that this kind of scientific knowledge leads to 'value judgements' – dangerous knowledge, in other words. Plomin replied that 'data doesn't dictate policy' – the findings themselves are simply neutral evidence, and so it is up to policy-makers how, if at all, it is used to shape policy. What this episode shows is the extent to which, even in areas where one might hope policy would be dictated by the evidence, this is not always the case. Muddled notions about fairness and equality often seem to stand in the way of clear thinking. The report by Cummings, quoted above, was an attempt to work out a policy that could best exploit the talents of the brightest children (the most important resource of British, and every other society) regardless of background. But it fell foul of an embedded political correctness.

Michael Young was writing at a time when it was more or less assumed that IQ was randomly distributed but, it turns out, that might not be exactly how it works: brainy types, it seems, have a better-than-average chance of having brainy children. So who gets to the top in a meritocracy is not mere chance – the genetic dice are loaded in favour of the offspring of those already on top of the pile; the top of today are, if you like, breeding the top of tomorrow. We seem to have arrived at that most paradoxical of situations – a hereditary meritocracy. And the mating behaviour of well-educated meritocrats is reinforcing the trend. 'Assortative mating' is the jargon term that social psychologists give to the phenomenon, and what it boils down to is that well-educated women tend to choose well-educated men as their marriage partners.

That might seem a very normal outcome, but it was not always so; back in the 1950s there were many more unions where one partner's educational level was much lower than the other (a fact partly explained by the disparity in higher educational levels between men and women – fewer women got to go to university in those days). Nevertheless, assortative mating naturally increases the likelihood that well-educated parents will have intelligent children. There's another factor too: the well-educated naturally value learning and so invest heavily in the education of their offspring. Taken altogether, the playing field begins to look far from level for any child not born into these propitious circumstances.

Bearing all this in mind, what connection is this likely to have with the BBC's outlook on the world? In the average

BBC newsroom there will be many above-average people; they will be much better-educated than most of the population and they will mostly come from comfortable middle-class backgrounds. Nearly everyone will have a degree and, as previously discussed, it is clear that the more highly educated the individual, the more likely it is that they voted Remain. The BBC's hostility to Brexit is thus revealed as no mystery, but rather, a logical outcome; it is exactly what the data would predict. This presents a huge difficulty to an organisation publicly dedicated to 'impartiality', because how can it fairly represent the views of the country when it is staffed by individuals who overwhelmingly favour one side of the argument? This is not to say that BBC journalists do not strive to overcome this problem – I believe most do, and do so valiantly – but it is very difficult to discount one's own opinions and put the same value on them as the other bloke's. The plain fact is that underlying convictions inevitably colour the everyday editorial decisions made by BBC journalists and programme makers.

Among Remainers there is an airy assumption, frequently made in private (though only rarely voiced in public), that the fact that the better-educated largely favoured staying in the EU shows the wisdom of their position. They are 'right' and the fact that a majority of the cleverest are on their side proves the wisdom of their case. Such a view is obviously consoling to crestfallen Remainers but Dominic Cummings, the mastermind of the Leave campaign, has a sharp rejoinder. They might be better educated, he says, but they are also more susceptible to social pressure from within their own group; education, he maintains, does not necessarily lead to independent thought, but rather a fashion-driven 'group-think'. Here's what he wrote on a long *Spectator* blog from January 2017 – his fullest exposition yet of his thoughts on what happened on 23 June 2016:

> I've learned over the years that 'rational discussion' accomplishes almost nothing in politics, particularly with people better educated than average. Most educated people are not set up to listen or change their minds about politics.

Before dismissing this as a snide put-down of that section of the population that was least receptive of Cumming's Brexit pitch, it is worth examining what at first sight seems an alarming – and deeply counter-intuitive – view. Professor Jennifer Hochschild of Harvard University has spent her professional lifetime studying voting patterns in American elections. Her latest book *Do Facts Matter? Information and Misinformation in American Politics*[2] concludes that people tend to avoid facts that contradict their beliefs while accepting affirmative

---

2   Jennifer L. Hochschild and Katherine Levine Einstein, *Do Facts Matter?: Information and Misinformation in American Politics* (University of Oakland Press, 2016).

facts automatically. Despite the common assumption that the better-educated are more sceptical and inquiring, or in other words, more open to a fact-based approach to politics, her research shows the opposite to be true. Interviewed about her work she says:

> Some evidence shows that people with more education are more likely to cling to their beliefs, so education is certainly not a panacea.

The explanation, she says, lies in an understanding of group dynamics. Mankind is a social animal and group belonging is a fundamental instinct; even questioning an established idea can threaten the individual's membership of the group:

> For example, if a member of a liberal group questioned whether global warming is a problem, she would have to question whether she can still be a good Democrat, perhaps stop talking, at least about this issue, to her colleagues and others in her class and peer groups.

There is, as yet, relatively little good British research into this area – maybe it is uncomfortable for academics to investigate so close to home. But there is plenty of anecdotal evidence from the current British academic scene which demonstrates a depressing herd instinct among the ivory towers. Take, for instance, the extraordinary row which has riven Oxford University's history faculty. It centres on Nigel Biggar, professor of moral and pastoral theology at Christ Church. In the autumn of 2017 Professor Biggar wrote an article in *The Times* which argued that the British Empire was neither wholly good nor wholly bad; his nuanced critique was that we should not need to feel quite so guilty about having been colonial masters of half the known world. His article was prompted by the work of another academic, Professor Bruce Gilley of Portland State University in Oregon who, in an article for the *Third World Quarterly*, questioned whether Western colonialism deserved its bad reputation. His heretical view is that many countries in the world were much better run, and their people much better treated, when they were part of the British Empire.

For both men the consequences of writing these articles has been dramatic. In Professor Gilley's case publication was followed by the dismal spectacle of the usual cyber-mob hate campaign; he was inevitably labelled a 'racist', and angry student demonstrations now follow him around. In Professor Biggar's case, sixty of his colleagues in Oxford's history faculty immediately denounced him in an open letter to *The Times*. In true Orwellian style they said he had been asking 'the wrong questions' – an odd thing for inquirers after historical truth to assert for, taken literally. It would seem to drastically limit academic inquiry. And anyway, who gets to define the 'right' questions?

So oppressive has the intellectual climate become within British universities that some of those few academics who self-identify as right-wing in outlook have been stirred to join a pressure group, the Heterodox Academy. It was set up by academics in the US and a number of British university teachers have since signed up. On its website it says that to solve those problems that trigger political passions, diversity of viewpoint is essential. The authors write:

> The surest sign that a community suffers from a deficit of viewpoint diversity is the presence of orthodoxy, most readily apparent when members fear shame, ostracism, or any other form of social retaliation for questioning or challenging a commonly held idea … The question, then, is whether colleges and universities welcome and celebrate viewpoint diversity.

The Heterodox Academy says that many US campuses now demonstrate an ideological monoculture which is damaging academic inquiry. They have a graph on their website[3] illustrating just how bad the situation has become; based on regular polling data from academic staff, it shows three lines denoting support for left wing, centrist and conservative positions. After decades of steadily dwindling support, only about

---

3   For more, see: https://heterodoxacademy.org/the-problem/

12 per cent of US academics now support the right, more than 60 per cent the left. British institutions are coy about this kind of polling so there is nothing like the same wealth of data available, however what there is tells much the same story. An online survey of academics carried out by the *Times Educational Supplement* before the 2015 general election found a mere 11 per cent saying they would be voting Conservative, 46 per cent said they would vote Labour, 22 per cent Green and 9 per cent Liberal Democrat. A researcher at Nuffield College, Oxford compared these results with findings published in a book by the Oxford sociologist A. H. Halsey in 1992, which tabulated political support among academics from the 1960s onwards. In 1965, he reports, 35 per cent of university teachers surveyed supported the Tories, falling to 29 per cent ten years later and 18 per cent by 1989. Though the earlier data was not like for like with the *TES* survey, the direction of travel is very clear: Britain's university teachers, overwhelmingly, incline to the left.

This matters, particularly in the context of the BBC's news and current affairs output. There used to be an old joke among *Today* producers that if you bagged a professor (or a bishop!) for a live interview on the story, it was job done. The relationship between the BBC's current affairs programmes and the academic world is a close one; naturally enough, when producers want an objective viewpoint they turn to academics who are, after all, attested experts in their field. But the fact that so many academics are left-leaning inevitably undermines claims of objectivity, particularly on subjects which are politically charged (and these are, obviously, the topics the BBC most wants to talk about). On a subject like Brexit a large majority of university teachers will have been Remain voters; among the BBC's own journalists, nearly all of them graduates, there will also have been a massive preponderance of Remainers. There is an intellectual symbiosis between the BBC and academia; they need each other and, what's more, they like each other. One illustration of this relationship is the number of BBC people who have gone on to head up Oxbridge colleges after leaving the Corporation: currently there are six.

And, returning to the matter of meritocrats, another factor is in play. Higher education increases feelings of self-worth; for the very highly educated this translates often into an ill-concealed sense of superiority. That very sense of superiority bolsters their sense of the rightness of their opinions – after all, they're educated. These people are naturally much less likely to have malleable political views because their high qualifications give them confidence in their opinions. Less well-educated people, on the other hand, approach political topics with more humility. Some of them will be open to persuasion by their better educated neighbours, precisely because they suffer from a sense of inferiority. On a subject like Brexit it is therefore no surprise at all that the BBC finds it so difficult to be truly impartial.

The BBC is Michael Young's 'word made flesh'; it is the meritocracy incarnate. It is an organisation whose staff are, overwhelmingly, drawn from a particular strata of society – the meritocratic elite – and that strata are becoming ever more ossified in terms of social mobility. If you are born to parents who themselves rose through their own 'merit', the likelihood is that you too will rise in the same way – you will have had a good education and certificates to prove your own 'merit'. So we have ended up with another variation on our traditional class structure – with the difference that this one can be defended more easily. It is easy to ridicule a system where dim aristocrats get to rule by virtue of the 'lucky sperm' lottery – much easier to justify one where those on top are told they deserve to be there by right of their 'merit'. This is not a system which encourages humility. This wouldn't matter so much for the BBC were it not for the fact that, along with membership of this class, goes a set of assumptions and values that turns out identikit opinions: that the better educated are less open-minded, in political terms, is an important and only partly explored phenomenon. But it is this fact, above all else, that might well be the explanation as to why the views of the BBC are so distinct – and so often out of step with the rest of the country.

CHAPTER FOUR

———————

NOT ONE OF US

AMONG THE MASSED RANKS of the BBC's approximately 5,000 journalists – making it one of the world's biggest employers of journalistic labour – there is a distinct hierarchy of esteem, and at the top of the tree are the foreign correspondents. The BBC takes foreign news very seriously; it boasts the most extensive network of news bureaux of any news-gathering organisation and it regards reporting the world as a sacred duty. Providing a reliable, fair and accurate record of what is happening in the world is the very core of the BBC's mission. How odd it is then, that since 2017, it should have so spectacularly fallen short of its own ideals when reporting on events from the Western world's most important capital city, Washington.

The election of Donald Trump as the 45th President of the United States of America in November 2016 was a watershed moment for the US and the world. The advent of every new presidency is self-evidently an important moment, but Trump's elevation marked a decisive break with seventy years of US political tradition: for the first time in post-war America the voters had put a real political outsider in the Oval Office, someone who won despite starting the campaign without the endorsement of either the Republican or Democratic parties. His victory posed the sternest possible test for the BBC's doctrine of impartiality, because Trump represents all that the BBC most dislikes.

After the cerebral, cool, progressive Obama – a man very much to the BBC's liking – Trump challenged the BBC's world view in the most obvious ways: he rejected the consensus on anthropogenic global warming (a theory which the BBC has elevated to a status beyond challenge), he made disparaging remarks about foreigners, talked of building walls to keep Mexican immigrants out and he said he wanted to restrict Muslim immigration to the US. And because Trump's positions on all these matters ran counter to the BBC's deepest instincts, it was inevitable that the Corporation's vaunted impartiality would be put to the test. In this context it is worth considering just what impartiality means: the Oxford Living Dictionary has it as: 'Equal treatment of all rivals or disputants; fairness'. And here is what the BBC itself says about it in its published editorial guidelines:

Impartiality lies at the heart of public service and is the core of the BBC's commitment to its audiences. It applies to all our output and services – television, radio, online, and in our international services and commercial magazines. We must be inclusive, considering the broad perspective and ensuring the existence of a range of views is appropriately reflected. The agreement accompanying the BBC charter requires us to do all we can to ensure controversial subjects are treated with due impartiality in our news and other output dealing with matters of public policy or political or industrial controversy. But we go further than that, applying due impartiality to all subjects … Due impartiality is often more than a simple matter of 'balance' between opposing viewpoints. Equally, it does not require absolute neutrality on every issue or detachment from fundamental democratic principles. The BBC Agreement forbids our output from expressing the opinion of the BBC on current affairs or matters of public policy, other than broadcasting or the provision of online services.

This is very noble stuff. Any democracy that has a public information source which lives up to the above description has a treasure beyond price; it means public debates can be conducted in full knowledge of the facts, with the voters fully informed and without being subjected to insidious bias. With a service like this a country gives itself the best possible chance of making good decisions. But how well, in practice, does the BBC measure up to this exacting standard? In particular, how fair has its reporting of President Trump been?

Let us start with a general observation; as a rule the BBC has more sympathy with the Democratic Party than the Republican Party. There are good reasons for this. Firstly, the Democrats are the champions of liberal opinion; their position on everything from healthcare to education to gender issues chimes with that of the BBC. The Republicans, on the other hand, have been foot-draggers when it comes to the 'progressive' agenda. Secondly, in the post-war period, the Democrats have usually (not always) been the more outward looking of the two parties – more willing to engage with the world and to acknowledge America's obligation to uphold the global system. From a British perspective, a Democrat administration in Washington usually makes for a more comfortable relationship in international affairs. Donald Trump's mantra of 'America First' is an explicit repudiation of that tradition of engagement which makes London nervous. The conventional Foreign Office view is that a Democrat President is usually preferable to a Republican, and the BBC agrees. However, this general predisposition towards the Democrats cannot wholly explain the naked hostility that the BBC displayed towards Trump from the outset of his term in office.

Immediately after his inauguration in mid-January 2017, President Trump announced his priorities. Prominent among them was his desire to limit immigration by building a wall along the border with Mexico and by freezing immigration from seven majority-Muslim countries. The Mexican wall issue is a long-term aspiration for Trump, but slowing the inflow from the seven named Muslim countries was something he thought he could act on without delay; he issued an executive order aimed at stopping all immigration from those countries for ninety days. Trump said he was acting in the interests of national security; his ostensible reason for the freeze on arrivals was to allow immigration authorities to carry out more detailed background checks on individuals to see if they posed a threat.

Trump's approach should have come as no surprise to anyone; during the presidential campaign he had spoken repeatedly of his desire to limit the arrival of more Muslims in the US so the travel ban he announced in January 2017 was an attempt to deliver on that campaign promise. In fact, it turned out to be far from straightforward for the President; a series of court rulings thwarted the imposition of the travel ban and it wasn't until June of 2017 that the US Supreme Court ruled that the proposed executive order was, in fact, constitutional, and even then what was granted was less than what Trump had wanted. But the travel ban proposal provoked a quite disproportionate response from the BBC.

Across BBC news outlets, from the *Ten O'Clock News*, to *Newsbeat* on Radio One, to the *World Service*, the travel ban was given top billing for days. In the Corporation's view this was news of major importance. On programme after programme experts were lined up to denounce the travel ban and to typify it as a nakedly discriminatory piece of legislation. On many shows there was no attempt to balance that kind of comment with anyone who actually thought the ban might have some merit. There is an obvious question which never seemed to be asked by any of these programmes which is: what did the voters think of a travel ban? But as so often is the case, the BBC judges matters according to its own priorities and prejudices while the wishes of ordinary citizens count for little if they fail to coincide with those of the Corporation.

It was left to researchers at Chatham House, aka the Royal Institute of International Affairs, the independent and well-respected London-based think tank, to settle the question; in February 2017 they asked 10,000 people from ten European countries whether they agreed or disagreed with the following statement: 'All further immigration from Muslim countries should be stopped'. The answer that came back was that, yes, they did agree with it. The actual figures were 55 per cent agreed, 25 per cent 'neither agreed nor disagreed' and only 20 per cent disagreed.[1] In other words, discounting those with no fixed opinion either way, Europeans in general were strongly

---

1   See: https://www.chathamhouse.org/expert/comment/what-do-europeans-think-about-muslim-immigration

of the opinion that they'd like to see no more Muslims allowed to settle in their countries.

The obvious inference to draw from the Chatham House poll was that although Trump was addressing American concerns, his proposals were very much in tune with what many European voters privately think. These poll findings should have informed BBC coverage of the issue, but they were resolutely ignored. Instead what followed was a deeply one-sided narrative which portrayed Muslims as an unfairly targeted minority group while entirely ignoring public opinion on the issue. As the BBC's editorial guidelines plainly state, the Corporation is not allowed to editorialise; in theory the BBC has no 'opinion' of its own. And it is true that you will never hear, see or read a news story authorised by the Corporation which starts: 'The BBC thinks…' However, there are much subtler ways of letting the audience know what you think than simply stating it in plain language. It was Robin Day, the BBC's grand inquisitor of a previous generation, who once remarked that 'Every question contains a comment', and it is true that the acute listener can usually infer the interviewer's own preference from the tone of the questioning. But, besides the tone of the interviewer, there is another obvious way in which the BBC shapes its news output to reflect its own values.

All journalism is a matter of selection. Every day there are literally thousands of stories which get reported somewhere or other. Via news agencies, newspapers, broadcasters and online sources these myriad stories pour into the BBC, but only a tiny fraction of them ever figure in the BBC's main news output. There are some stories, naturally, which cannot be excluded, and major world events, be they political, military or natural disasters will always make it into the news bulletin. But the bulk of the BBC's output is discretionary, by which I mean that someone, somewhere, has decided that one story deserves attention whereas another story does not. How these decisions are made will depend to a greater or lesser extent on the background, experience and – crucially – the political preferences of the person making the selection. The BBC cannot be expected to forego its right to discriminate in this way between stories (the audience rightly expects it to sieve through the day's news and to present them with the most important stories) but – as in the case of the 'Muslim travel ban' – an undue emphasis on any particular story can, objectively speaking, look lopsided and partisan.

The disproportionate amount of airtime that the BBC devoted to the 'Muslim travel ban' (as the story came to be known – perhaps confusingly, as Muslims from other countries were unaffected) went on for many weeks. When the initial furore died down and the BBC's US-based journalists turned their attentions to other aspects of the new administration's programme there was a pronounced tone of mocking hostility quite unlike anything I can ever remember from the BBC previously. It is true that in 1982, when he was first elected, the BBC was initially disdainful of Ronald Reagan; many BBC correspondents were disparaging about his B-movie film star career and his programme for government, but the snootiness faded quite quickly as his policies started to yield results.

There has been no sign of that with Trump. It is true, of course, that Trump offends metropolitan elites on both sides of the Atlantic, by virtue of his bumptiousness, boasting and vulgarity, and that his administration has sometimes seemed chaotic, but even so, the BBC's naked opposition demands explanation. Part of the reason might be the simple snobbery of sophisticated left-wing types who cannot abide the elevation of a man who they think is their intellectual (and moral) inferior. But that is only part of the story; the probable reason concerns the Corporation's fierce attachment to the idea of unfettered immigration. The BBC's support for continued mass immigration into the UK is one of those areas where its detachment from the concerns of the man in the street most clearly highlight the gulf between BBC 'anywheres' and its audience of 'somewheres'.

The identification of the left with permissive immigration policies has a long pedigree. It was the post-war Labour government of Clement Attlee which passed into law the 1948 British Nationality Act which gave all people living under British rule in other parts of the world the right to come and live in the UK; in theory, this high-minded and idealistic law gave right of entry to 800 million people to move to Britain, an insupportable and impractical idea. In practice, the authorities quickly began to find ways to prevent this happening (a favourite ploy, much used by British officials overseas, was to make it hard for people to acquire the necessary travel documents). In subsequent decades successor governments passed legislation rowing back from the original position, not least because, while Britain has always shown more tolerance to incomers than most countries, mass immigration has never been popular.

There is a point to be emphasised here, which is that British attitudes toward immigration and foreigners in general are a world away from the caricature presented by *The Guardian* and all too often echoed by the BBC. The oft-repeated and lazy depiction of the UK experiencing an upsurge in xenophobia is simply not borne out by the facts. One of the most thorough investigations of attitudes came from the US-based Pew Research Center, which in 2015 asked respondents in America and Europe a series of questions. Here is what they concluded about the UK:

> In the United Kingdom, by contrast, views toward immigrants are more uniformly positive. The U.K. is also home to a significant number of immigrants born outside of the EU (5.2 million). About half (52%) said immigrants are a strength, a share that trailed only Germany. At the

same time, just 20% in the U.K. said immigrants are more to blame for crime than other groups, among the lowest shares in Europe. On assimilation, about half (47%) said immigrants today want to be distinct from U.K. society.[2]

As a general observation there is a natural resistance on the part of host populations everywhere to the arrival in their midst of large numbers of newcomers. This is often ascribed to racism – properly defined as a belief in the superiority of one's own racial grouping and an antagonism to others – but labelling people as 'racist' is all too often used merely to justify ignoring their natural concerns. 'Racist' is a politically weaponised term of abuse designed to smear the opposition and close down the debate – for who can prove themselves innocent? Of course, 'racism' in its purest form might sometimes be present, but it is not the only, nor necessarily the most important factor: more relevant is the concept of xenophobia – a fear of foreigners. For, while all racists are xenophobes, not all xenophobes are racist. Xenophobia is an exaggerated fear or mistrust of that which is foreign and unfamiliar. It is often bracketed with racism, but the two should not be confused; they are quite distinct. For instance, it is quite possible that a white Briton and a black Briton might share a fear and mistrust of immigrants from,

---

2   Jens Manuel Krogstad, 'What Americans, Europeans think of immigrants', Pew Research Center, 24 September 2015.

say, Germany. That might make them xenophobes, but not necessarily racists; in fact, their fear is directed at someone of the same racial category – Caucasian. Xenophobia arises from a shared group identity (in this instance, being British), not from an exclusively racial identity.

Belonging to a group, identifying with the other individuals in it and protecting the perceived self-interest of the group are universal human attributes. This holds good as much for university lecturers as uneducated labourers – though only the first of these groups gets to set the terms of debate and condemn the attitude of the other.

The natural tendency towards group identity, combined with a fear of identifiably different outsiders, is a standing temptation to unscrupulous political operators. Appealing to the base instincts of the majority group, while denigrating and threatening a minority, is clearly immoral and wrong; but it is also wrong to suppress the legitimate concerns of the majority by dismissing them as crude 'racists', and yet this is what the BBC has done in a decades-long campaign facilitating mass immigration to Britain. A seminal moment came in 1968 when the Tory politician Enoch Powell delivered what came to be known as the 'Rivers of Blood' speech. Powell, then a member of Ted Heath's shadow Cabinet, was MP for Wolverhampton South West and thus someone who had first-hand experience of immigration – his constituency had seen large numbers of black immigrants in the previous decade. His speech, delivered in a Birmingham hotel,[3] foretold, in apocalyptic terms, of a Britain riven by racial conflict which would result in hideous strife and bloodshed.

His words had the powerful and immediate effect of elevating him to the position of people's champion – at least for that section of the public who agreed with him. It also effectively ended his career as a front-rank politician – Heath sacked him, and thereafter he was always a maverick figure delivering his philippics from the margins. In retrospect, it can be seen that Powell did a massive disservice to the immigration debate; his intemperate language and lurid imagery allowed his opponents to paint him as an unhinged and malevolent fantasist. He was immediately labelled a 'racist', although he always rejected that label; perhaps he was merely a xenophobe. Whatever, his problem was that he was a too florid rhetorician who alarmed Middle Britain with his nightmare vision. His anecdote about an old white lady who had human excrement pushed through her letterbox by black immigrants and his use of the racial slur, 'piccaninnies', were both crass and politically unintelligent; it made him a very easy target for those of his opponents who labelled him a straightforward racist. The British in general

---

3 Enoch Powell made his 'Rivers of Blood' speech on 20 April 1968 at the Midland Hotel, Birmingham, to an audience of Conservative Party activists. In April 2018 – on the fiftieth anniversary of the speech – the BBC broadcast a re-enactment on radio – the first time the Corporation had ever relayed the speech in full.

like politeness in their politicians – they do not appreciate public figures who speak too bluntly. The most significant result of his clumsy intervention was that it gave his opponents the pretext they needed to close down any meaningful debate for the next forty years.

After Powell's fateful speech his very name became a damning shorthand for anyone who spoke out of turn on immigration. The BBC was especially assiduous in conjuring up the spectre of the 'rivers of blood' whenever immigration matters entered the realm of political debate – which was rarely. And the reason it intruded so infrequently was because the BBC, and politicians of the left, did not want it discussed, and so allowed anyone who insisted on raising it to be smeared, damningly, as 'racist'. In 2007 Margaret Hodge, Labour MP for Barking in east London, penned an article for *The Guardian* headlined 'A message to my fellow immigrants', which finally spelled out something long suspected:

> In our open, tolerant society, there are, thankfully, few issues that remain taboo. But, motivated by the fear of both legitimising racism and encouraging the extreme right, migration is one.[4]

---

4   Margaret Hodge, 'A message to my fellow immigrants', *The Guardian*, 20 May 2007.

This is in many ways a remarkable statement which, with perfect clarity, explains why it is that the UK never had the honest immigration debate it so desperately needed. Because, isn't it rather obvious that determining who should and who should not be allowed to come and live in one of the most densely populated European countries is a central responsibility of government? But politicians of the left didn't want an immigration debate and, especially after the Powell speech, the BBC made sure they got their way. Of course the Corporation never explicitly endorsed the closing down of discussion on this sensitive topic, but its complicity with this doctrine of 'taboo' had a dramatically chilling effect on debate; politicians quickly learned that, for the BBC, immigration was a subject strictly off-limits. Failure to abide by the rules could be career-ending, which is why through the '70s, '80s and '90s and into the new century immigration was a subterranean issue, something discussed in the privacy of the pub or kitchen, but which politicians invoked at their peril. Meanwhile, throughout that period, the country was becoming home to increasingly large numbers of migrants.

The accession of the UK to the EEC in 1973 changed the dynamics of immigration to Britain; previously most immigrants had come from Commonwealth countries – the West Indies, Pakistan and India, in particular. But after '73 Britain was bound by a treaty commitment to freedom of movement between member countries. Over the next few decades large numbers of Europeans settled in Britain, many in London and other big metropolitan areas, and often arriving as highly skilled workers. The influx was barely noticed and caused few problems, but things changed after 2004. That was the year when ten countries – seven of them former Soviet satellites – acceded to the EU.

It was open to the existing EU member countries to impose temporary restrictions on the numbers allowed in from the new countries (this was allowed as a way of checking disruptive immigration flows) but Tony Blair's New Labour government decided not to enforce any restrictions. Consequently, Britain experienced a huge influx in a few short years. Census figures for Polish people in the UK (who represented a significant proportion of the incomers) give a flavour of what happened: in 2001 there were only 66,000 Polish-born UK residents – but by 2016 that figure had risen to 911,000 and the biggest rise in numbers came in the years 2005–2010. Overall, between 1997 and 2010 a total of 2.2 million people arrived and settled in the UK.

Immigration started to be a serious problem for the Blair government from the mid-noughties onwards. Having been off-limits for years, immigration suddenly surfaced as a hot political topic because many Labour MPs started experiencing a backlash and were forced to begin talking about it. That, finally, legitimised the subject for the BBC. A significant moment came in 2006 when the Labour MP for

Southampton Itchen, John Denham, wrote a private memo (which only came to light years later) to Blair and Brown setting out what had happened in his area. In June 2012 Mr Denham, then an adviser to Labour leader Ed Miliband, was asked when he felt that immigration had got out of control and replied: 'I think for me in really 2005. It was then it became clear that the estimates we relied on were vastly wrong'. In March 2015 *The Guardian* revealed the existence of Mr Denham's memo in a long investigative article about Labour's immigration policies. He had said that 14,000 Eastern Europeans had settled in Southampton in the previous eighteen months and that many of them were self-employed builders. He said this had huge repercussions for the construction trades so that the daily rate for a builder, he claimed, had fallen by 50 per cent; it had also impacted hospital and other services. He cited the case of a local FE college which had had to close its doors after 1,000 people tried to sign up in a single day for its English-as-a-second-language course.

The public started taking note and political alarm bells were ringing to the extent that the following year, in his first address to the Labour Party conference as Prime Minister, Gordon Brown pledged that in future his government's priority would be 'British jobs for British workers' (a much-mocked sound bite because under EU freedom of movement rules any such policy would be illegal). Supporters of permissive immigration policies often argue that immigration is an unalloyed economic good – though it's worth remembering who it is that's saying this; there are very few jobs in university senior common rooms, economic research outfits or BBC newsrooms that are competed for by recently arrived immigrants. The people who feel the ill-effects of low-skilled migrants, are low-skilled indigenous workers who experience downward pressure on their pay and increased competition for housing, schooling and a range of other services. In the noughties, immigration was usually presented in public debate as the benevolent by-product of a booming economy – but there was a political subtext too. Andrew Neather, a policy adviser at the Home Office and a sometime-speech writer to Tony Blair, rather let the cat out of the bag when he wrote a piece for the *Evening Standard* in 2009. Recalling meetings with his political masters he wrote:

> I remember coming away from some discussions with the clear sense that the policy was intended – even if this wasn't its main purpose – to rub the Right's nose in diversity and render their arguments out of date.[5]

The key word to note here is 'diversity' which comes freighted with good intentions; diversity, in the eyes of the left, is always

---

5   Andrew Neather, 'Don't listen to the whingers – London needs immigrants', *Evening Standard*, 23 October 2009.

a good thing – and you can't have too much of it. This has been the stance of progressives throughout the Western world; it is often argued that diversity brings economic benefits and yet, interestingly, not every country has followed this road. Japan, one of the most successful economies in the world, is also one of the least diverse. In their case homogeneity seems to have done them no harm – while, incidentally, making them one of the few places in the world to have escaped Islamic terrorism. But in Britain, progressives like Mr Neather were part of a New Labour drive – carried out surreptitiously and against the instincts of the people – to facilitate mass immigration. And what is more, Mr Neather thinks this was a thoroughly good thing because it made cheap labour available to the middle classes:

> It didn't just happen: the deliberate policy of ministers from late 2000 until at least February last year, when the Government introduced a points-based system, was to open up the UK to mass migration … The results in London, and especially for middle-class Londoners, have been highly positive. It's not simply a question of foreign nannies, cleaners and gardeners – although frankly it's hard to see how the capital could function without them. Their place certainly wouldn't be taken by unemployed BNP voters from Barking or Burnley – fascist au pair, anyone? Immigrants are everywhere and in all sorts of jobs, many of them skilled.

Mr Neather was one of the few people who were in the know about this government policy; though he was later to claim that there had been no conspiracy to hasten the realisation of a multicultural society, the taboo on public debate about immigration meant that the public remained largely in the dark. When it started to dawn on the voters what had been going on there was a reaction and Labour politicians, like Margaret Hodge, began a rear-guard action to try to reassure native British voters that their interests, not only those of the newcomers, would henceforth also be taken into account. In Ms Hodge's aforementioned article, 'A message to my fellow immigrants', she frankly admits:

> We prioritise the needs of an individual migrant family over the entitlement others feel they have. So a recently arrived family with four or five children living in a damp and overcrowded, privately rented flat with the children suffering from asthma will usually get priority over a family with less housing need who have lived in the area for three generations and are stuck at home with the grandparents.

And she made a half promise:

> We should look at policies where the legitimate sense of entitlement felt by the indigenous family overrides the legitimate need demonstrated by the new migrants.

But time was running out for New Labour, and by the 2010 general election immigration had become an issue where they were extremely vulnerable. In the run-up to the election David Cameron, pledged that a government under his leadership would bring net immigration down to the 'tens of thousands' rather than the hundreds of thousands who had year by year been swelling the country's population. It was a meaningless promise, pounced on by Eurosceptics, because the terms of the EU treaty guaranteeing freedom of movement meant no British government, whatever its stated intentions, could legally impede the inward flow of EU migrants. However, it was a powerful campaign message, and one that helped the Tories to garner enough votes to go into government, albeit in coalition with the pro-immigration Liberal Democrats.

This long digression into the history of the British debate on immigration is relevant because it illustrates the way in which left-leaning politicians and the BBC conspired to make it, as Margaret Hodge accurately labelled it a 'taboo' subject. It is, surely, rather odd that the BBC should consider any subject a taboo (strictly defined as something prohibited by social custom), but it is nevertheless the case that immigration was one of a select few subjects which for decades the BBC would not talk about. When it came to other taboos held by a previous generation – essentially taboos concerning sex – the BBC was eager to dismantle the restrictions. From the 1970s onwards the BBC was at the forefront of a campaign by progressives to subvert all taboos about sex – a process now, in all essentials, complete – while simultaneously upholding and enforcing the taboo on debating immigration – and, by extension, race.

Here we get close to the essence of the 'noble lie' that the BBC has been perpetuating: that by not talking about immigration, by ruling all debate about the subject illegitimate, it believed it was helping to ensure social harmony. In the face of a huge increase in the number of foreigners entering the country the BBC decided that silence was the best policy. It is also possible by looking at this particular 'noble lie' to see why this is a profoundly mistaken approach – as well as being at odds with the BBC's own credo of impartiality.

The BBC's suppression of a legitimate debate on immigration has, I believe, in part, ironically contributed to an outcome it deplores: Brexit. Suppose, for a moment, that the BBC had allowed an open debate from the 1970s onwards that would, very likely, have forced governments of all stripes to have been more explicit about immigration policy. It might very well have resulted in fewer immigrants moving to the UK, because there would have been political pressure to slow the inward flow. But it would have ensured that there was no sudden 'discovery' of the immigration debate as happened in the late noughties. By the time the immigration debate was dragged into the open the country had already experienced a very high rate of immigration with consequences not to everyone's liking. This was alarming to many people, and the desire to 'take back control' of the UK's borders was certainly one important factor in the Brexit debate. In addition to its being absolutely wrong for the BBC to make some subjects 'taboo', it is also, finally, counterproductive: the truth will out – and when it escapes its gaolers it can wreak political havoc. Pretending that things are other than they actually are is no recipe for social harmony, but rather a social time bomb. Moreover, it also leads to nonsensical journalism.

Take, for instance, the subject of housing. Over the past decade or so the question of how to ensure decent homes for all has steadily risen up the political agenda. The problems facing young people wanting to buy their own homes has been the subject of countless BBC interviews and investigations, and yet the obvious link between immigration and the housing shortage goes largely unmentioned. Between 2000 and 2016, according to official figures the UK's population grew by nearly seven million people. All those newcomers need somewhere to lay their heads at night, and so it seems no less than common sense to say that the housing shortage and immigration are connected. The most basic notion in economics is the link between prices and supply and demand: when demand rises, and supply doesn't keep up, prices rise. It would be simplistic (and wrong) to blame the housing shortage entirely on immigration; there are other complexities including, for instance, the fact that the shortage is not a uniform national phenomenon, and is mainly confined to housing hotspots. But the overall point holds good; the effects of mass immigration should inform every discussion of the housing crisis. However, the BBC has steadfastly ignored it because its gives ammunition for those who argue that immigration should be slowed. The clear and obvious link between immigration and the housing shortage remains one of the great unmentionables.

The BBC is still loath to encourage real debate on immigration, which is part of the reason that it is so manifestly hostile to Donald Trump. The US President is plain-speaking to the point of crude, and nowhere more so than on the subject of immigration. On this issue he speaks to the deepest concerns of his political base; his voters want America to remain a majority-white and Christian country; they do not share a vision of the US as an increasingly multicultural *mélange*. This puts them at odds with a liberal-left organisation like the BBC as much as with liberals in the USA itself. One can argue the rights and wrongs of the underlying divisions – the liberal vision of a world where all tribal identities have been subsumed in a universal brotherhood of mankind is a beguiling, though utopian, one – but there is no doubt on which side the BBC places itself. And the Corporation applies the same calculus to every world leader; that is why it deplores Viktor Orbán in Hungary and Jarosław Kaczyński of Poland and why one of its former darlings – Aung San Suu Kyi of Myanmar – has now fallen from grace.

The BBC has a very rigid code when it comes to immigration and race relations; its Manichaean view of these subjects has led it to a position quite at odds with its supposed role as impartial arbiter. This is not to argue that the BBC ever could, or should, be on the side of racists or give racism a platform, but it is to make the point that the fears of majority populations in the face of rapid demographic change are legitimate and embedded in our human nature. People who object to large numbers of foreigners coming into the country and changing its character should not be instantly accused of racism; a small number of them probably are racist, but the majority of them are more likely to be expressing normal human concerns.

The UK's current anxieties over immigration are due to the suddenness of the influx; they're analogous to the feeling of indigestion people suffer when they eat too much. In a well-regulated diet, when you eat enough and no more, you don't notice the processes of the gut; but when you eat too much your gut rebels. As Britain has shown over many decades, there is a high tolerance of immigration – but the rate at which the newcomers arrive is a critical factor. Like a digestive system overloaded with too much food, a country which is forced to absorb too many people too quickly is likely to experience a reaction. This is exactly what has happened in Germany because of Chancellor Angela Merkel's well-intentioned but politically disastrous decision to throw open the country's borders to mass immigration in 2015. The Blair government's reckless expansion of immigration, which was pursued for disreputable political motives, has made immigration toxic. The BBC's complicity in covering up the subject means it too must shoulder part of the blame. Its noble lie – that immigration at whatever level is a good thing – has harmed community relations. In short, the BBC, driven by a dogmatic liberal idealism, has taken sides in dereliction of its own charter obligations and at the cost of distorting a crucial national debate.

CHAPTER FIVE

AUNTIE THE APOSTATE: LOSING HER RELIGION

THE TENDENCY OF THE BBC to identify with, and then champion, progressive opinion can be traced back almost to its earliest beginnings; the notion of Broadcasting House being a nest of lefties was being aired by conservatives as far back as the 1930s. But at least until the 1960s there were countervailing influences at work in the higher reaches of BBC management. Partly, this was due to the long incumbency of John Reith as the BBC's first Director-General, a role he fulfilled from 1927 to 1938. There was nothing remotely 'progressive' about Reith's world view; born in 1889, just when Imperial Britain was nearing the apogee of its power and influence, he was formed by the strict tenets of Calvinist theology. Reith was the son of a Presbyterian minister and throughout his long life (he died in 1971) he never publicly deviated from support for a conventional Christian morality, and he carried this same moral high-mindedness into his work at the BBC. Reith had a vision of the BBC as fulfilling a higher public purpose and ensured that broadcasting in the UK followed a quite different trajectory than in other countries.

In the latter stages of WWI Reith worked for the British Army in the United States in an arms procurement role. This followed a stint soldiering on the front line where he was recognised as a courageous, sometimes to the point of foolhardy, officer; the stern cragginess of his features, which stare out from the many portrait photos, are accentuated by the bullet wound which removed a large chunk of his left cheek in 1915. His time in America exposed him to the infant radio industry which was in the process of realising the medium's potential for entertainment; popular music and live relays from sporting events were beginning to enlist big audiences and make money for the industry. When he took charge of the British Broadcasting Company in 1922, as general manager, Reith had a quite different vision for the future of radio. From the outset he consciously envisaged the BBC as an instrument of moral improvement for the nation; even before the BBC became a public corporation he ensured its purposes were not dominated only by commercial concerns. The first Royal Charter granted in 1927 (when the organisation ceased to be a private company) talks of 'the great value of such services as a means of disseminating information, education and entertainment'; so the higher purpose was given priority over mere frivolity.

In those early years of the BBC's existence, its corporate character first took shape: it was serious-minded, consciously aligned with traditional Christian morality and conscious also of its obligation to be fair. The potential of radio as a counterweight to the influence of newspapers and also the dangers they could pose in the hands of unscrupulous propagandists had early been recognised by politicians. So from its beginnings the Corporation applied scrupulous attention to the need for even-handedness. But everything it did in those days was in the context of an agreed national understanding that certain things were taken for granted and not to be questioned: the monarchy, the constitution, the British Empire, the League of Nations and, most importantly, Christianity – all these were the agreed backdrop to the BBC's world.

As noted in Chapter Two, the Second World War represented a special kind of challenge for the Corporation. For while the BBC as an institution, and individual BBC employees themselves, undoubtedly felt the same patriotic loyalty as other people, the organisation, and its staff, were bound by the obligation they felt to be truth tellers. In the first years of its existence, the BBC set itself the task of becoming a source of information trusted by everyone, which, even in peacetime, is a supremely difficult task. There were early tests: the general strike of 1926 – before the BBC even became a public corporation – found the BBC accused of siding with the government for not allowing the strikers to make their appeal directly to the country. So it was obvious that 'truth telling' was always going to be controversial and difficult and would involve very delicate judgements. Telling the truth during wartime was an even more exacting challenge because it called for making judgements about what information might properly be revealed and what might imperil national safety. 'Telling the truth' under such circumstances should be seen as something quite radical; something, as the novelist Penelope Fitzgerald declared, never before attempted. So the BBC can take pride that the judgement of history has been that the organisation met the challenge, insofar as that was possible, and emerged with its reputation for truthfulness enhanced.

Right in the middle of the war, at what might, without exaggeration, be called 'the darkest hour', the BBC broadcast a series of remarkable talks by the writer C. S. Lewis. The first instalment was originally billed as 'Broadcast Talks' (1942), then came 'Christian Behaviour' (1943) and finally 'Beyond Personality' (1944), but the whole lot taken altogether came to be published in book form in 1952 as *Mere Christianity*.[1] At a distance, now more than seven decades old, one thing that strikes the modern reader is the quite unselfconscious way the BBC saw fit to broadcast a

---

1 *Mere Christianity* has never been out of print since its first publication in 1952.

series of talks about Christian apologetics as if this was the most natural thing in the world. Which, at the time, it was, because underpinning the whole idea of this country's involvement in the war was the idea that it was a fight which pitted light against dark, truth against lies. For Lewis, that same conflict lies at the heart of the Christian faith and it is very telling that the wartime BBC felt it could wholeheartedly and unblushingly embrace the analysis he proffered.

C. S. Lewis today is probably best known as the author of that captivating series of children's books set in the imagined land of Narnia. The seven books in the series – collectively *The Chronicles of Narnia* – draw their inspiration from a multitude of classical sources, but the whole is infused with a robust Christian ethic: the children in the adventures face trials and tribulations which challenge their consciences and, though it is done with a light touch, the reader is left in no doubt about what is right and what is wrong. In *Mere Christianity* Lewis approached the same subject but much more explicitly, and for an adult readership. Lewis himself had been raised in a Church of Ireland[2] household in Belfast, but though he had rejected Christianity in adolescence he came back to it in his early thirties after a long intellectual struggle. He was a learned man who held the chair in Medieval and Renaissance English

---

2   The Church of Ireland is the Anglican Church of Ireland and should not be confused with Presbyterianism, a quite different Christian tradition.

at Cambridge University for many years, as well as a fiction writer of genius; he was also a sincere and believing Christian. In his introduction to *Mere Christianity* he describes himself, with becoming modesty as:

> a very ordinary layman of the Church of England, not especially 'high', nor especially 'low' nor especially anything else. But in this book I am not trying to convert anyone to my own position. Ever since I became a Christian I have thought that the best, perhaps the only, service I could do for my unbelieving neighbours, was to explain and defend the belief that has been common to nearly all Christians, at all times.

What follows is a series of short talks – thirty-three in all – which, though using simple and direct language (there is none of the confusing and obfuscatory jargon of the professional philosopher), dwell on the most profound questions which face human beings. Lewis's high intelligence and clarity of thought and expression allow him to penetrate effortlessly the very heart of these questions. So, for instance, he adduces the idea of a moral law known to all human beings which allows them, instinctively, to tell right from wrong. Placing this in a then contemporary setting he writes that both Christians and atheists know that what Hitler was doing was wrong, hence immoral. This moral law, he says, operates at the humdrum level too: all people, atheists and believers alike, know that stealing is wrong. He extends the idea positing a universal moral law which he says is like a law of nature because it is not a man-made construct, but understood intuitively. But, he says, unlike the other laws of nature governing the physical world, the moral law can be ignored. So that, whereas none of us can defy the law of gravity, every individual decides for themselves whether to obey the precepts of the moral law, by, for instance, stealing or not stealing. Here is his concluding thought on the matter:

> These, then, are the two points that I wanted to make. First, that human beings, all over the earth, have this curious idea that they ought to behave in a certain way, and cannot really get rid of it. Secondly, that they do not in fact behave in that way. They know the Law of Nature; they break it. These two facts are the foundation of all clear thinking about ourselves and the universe we live in.

At the centre of the talks is Lewis's profound insight when contemplating the character of Jesus Christ himself. He contrives a 'proof' that Jesus is truly who he says he is (i.e. the Son of God) by contriving what came to be called the 'Lewis Trilemma'.[3] He writes that there are three possibilities when

---

3 This was not, in fact, an original thought; earlier Christian apologists also argued in this way.

considering Jesus: either he is who he claims to be, or he is lying, or he is delusional – that is to say he was a madman who imagined himself to be God. Lewis then considers what we know of Jesus's character through the gospel stories and concludes that the last two possibilities are inconsistent with the written record and that, consequently, Jesus is what he claimed to be. Christianity, in other words, is true:

> I am trying here to prevent anyone saying the really foolish thing that people often say about Him: 'I'm ready to accept Jesus as a great moral teacher, but I don't accept his claim to be God.' That is the one thing we must not say. A man who was merely a man and said the sort of things Jesus said would not be a great moral teacher. He would either be a lunatic – on the level with the man who says he is a poached egg – or else he would be the Devil of Hell. You must make your choice. Either this man was, and is, the Son of God, or else a madman or something worse. You can shut him up for a fool, you can spit at him and kill him as a demon or you can fall at his feet and call him Lord and God, but let us not come with any patronising nonsense about his being a great human teacher. He has not left that open to us. He did not intend to.

The talks, and the subsequently published book of the talks, had a deep and long-lasting impact. It is not possible to know how many individual lives have been changed by *Mere Christianity*, but it has been widely recognised as a hugely influential work. There are many converts – many unknown, but some famous like the Battle of Britain ace pilot Leonard Cheshire VC and the economist E. F. Schumacher – who attribute their conversion directly to Lewis's writings. In the year 2000 the readership of *Christianity Today*, the leading journal of Evangelical Christianity in the US, voted *Mere Christianity* as the best book of the twentieth century. All of which is merely to point out that while the BBC could have had no inkling of the impact the talks would have, it did not shy away from the idea of granting Lewis lots of scarce airtime to promote an explicitly Christian message. This was an example of the BBC directly abetting evangelism through the medium of its airwaves, which tells us something important about the climate of internal opinion at the BBC in the 1940s. Reith might have gone – but his spirit still permeated the corridors of Broadcasting House.

Lewis's talks were not universally welcomed, certainly not among his colleagues at Oxford University. In 1947 *Time* magazine did a cover story on (the increasingly famous) Lewis with the reporter noting that he was regarded as an academic 'heretic' for believing in God. Some Oxford contemporaries regarded Lewis as having contracted a form of religious mania, and there is at least some evidence that his role as a radio evangelist damaged his academic career; his elder brother Warne is

quoted saying that he was surprised on discovering 'the viru-
lence of the anti-Christian feeling at Oxford'. In 1951 one don
admitted voting against Lewis being granted the prestigious
poetry chair, precisely because he had written works of popular theology (he lost that vote by 194 to 173). That anti-Lewis,
and by extension, anti-Christian sentiment was already firmly
established in university circles and was only to grow stronger
in succeeding decades. And nowhere did it flourish more
vigorously, nor have a more damaging impact, than within
the BBC.

What happened in post-war Britain to so dramatically
undermine Christianity's place at the centre of national affairs?
It is a largely untold and unexamined story and one in which
the BBC plays a leading role. Firstly, it should be said that the
collapse in the prestige, influence and centrality of Christianity
in Britain was not a sudden, unheralded event. The growing
confidence and visibility of a publicly proclaimed atheism was
in evidence for many decades previously. Matthew Arnold had
penned his famous lines on the modern world's loss of faith
nearly eighty years earlier in his 1867 poem 'Dover Beach'. The
fourth stanza begins:

> The Sea of Faith
> Was once too, at the full, and round earth's shore
> Lay like the folds of a bright girdle furled.
> But now I only hear

Its melancholy, long, withdrawing roar,
Retreating, to the breath
Of the night-wind, down the vast edges drear
And naked shingles of the world

Many arguments have been adduced as to why this turning away from God began and none can be conclusive, but the explanation surely lies in a combination of factors that shaped the modern world from the time of the industrial revolution onwards. The industrial revolution was itself the lusty off-spring of the Enlightenment when rationality, that is the power of human reason, challenged the supremacy of religion. But whereas the Enlightenment was a matter for philosophers, scientists and thinkers, the industrial revolution that came in its train affected everyone. Before that time – let us say the mid-eighteenth century – technological progress had been steady, but relatively slow, and the way in which the everyday lives of the mass of people were changed by technology had been gradual. But the great leap forward that began in Britain sometime around 1760 supercharged the process.

Machine manufacturing, the creation of new factories, new methods, materials and processes swept up increasing numbers of people into this new world. It brought prosperity to many and misery to many others, but in a wider sense, it demonstrated the increasing ingenuity of mankind; every year, decade on decade, new wonders were unveiled – each a testament to human cleverness. People, first in Britain, but later in other countries as they, too, industrialised, mastered the natural world in new ways. They became less subject to nature and its vagaries, ever more in control of their environment. And, in link step with this industrial advance, went scientific discovery; new ideas, like Darwin's theory of evolution (*On the Origin of Species* was published in 1859), entered the discourse and began to undermine traditional beliefs. Religion still held an honoured position through the High Victorian era in Britain but increasingly, in the new century, it was rendered lip service only. The further and faster technology progressed, the more the national heart swelled with pride in human achievement. Who needs God when we have learned to fly?

The Great War, 1914–18, had a dual effect; for some it precipitated a loss of faith, for a smaller number, perhaps, the opposite; but what it incontrovertibly showed was the new destructive power now held by human hands. For many it gave weight to the Nietzschean adage that 'God is dead',[4] for how could God exist in a world where the horrors of mechanised slaughter had been made all too evident? The Second World

---

4 'God is dead': the phrase first appeared in Nietzsche's 1882 collection *Die fröhliche Wissenschaft* – literally 'The Gay Science' or 'The Joyful Pursuit of Knowledge and Understanding'. However, it is better known from its appearance in Nietzsche's *Thus Spoke Zarathustra*. Nietzsche's point is that post-Enlightenment, belief in God had become impossible, though it is worth noting that in the first instance he puts the words in the mouth of 'the madman'.

War, 1939–45, ending, as it did, in the dropping of atomic bombs on the Japanese cities of Nagasaki and Hiroshima, only reinforced that notion. The world that emerged from the ruins of that war was one where man had demonstrated a godlike capacity for destruction. The power to destroy the world itself was, seemingly, now in human hands; where once mankind was taught to fear God, now it learned to fear itself.

The late 1940s was a time of dramatic political change in Britain. In 1945 the great war leader Churchill was unceremoniously dumped by the voters in favour of Clement Attlee, who may have lacked Churchill's soaring rhetorical powers, but had a clear vision of how he wanted to transform the country, a vision shared by a majority in a war-weary country. What is more, he had a parliamentary majority of 146 with which to force change through. Nowadays, what tends to be most celebrated about the post-war Labour government is the inception of the welfare state, and in particular the National Health Service, the embodiment of an ideal socialised public service. What is less well known, indeed almost wholly overlooked, is the fact that it was an Archbishop of Canterbury, William Temple, who has a strong claim to be one of the intellectual godfathers of the welfare state. Indeed, the very term 'welfare state' was one he coined in a lecture in 1928.[5]

---

5   Scott Holland Memorial Lecture, 'Christianity and the State', University of Liverpool, 1928.

William Temple was a short-lived Archbishop of Canterbury; appointed in 1942, he died in 1944 to be replaced by Geoffrey Fisher whose incumbency then lasted right into the 1960s.

Temple's short term in office might be one of the reasons why his significance is so often overlooked. In the 1920s and 1930s there were many political thinkers who wrote extensively about improving the lot of the working class, but few contributions to the debate were as influential as Temple's *Christianity and Social Order*, published in 1942. It sold in astonishing quantities – 150,000 copies flew off the shelves – and it adumbrated many of the actual measures which Attlee's government introduced. In his book Temple advocated universal healthcare, education for all, decent social housing and improved working conditions – the core programme, in fact, of the new government. It would be an exaggeration to claim Temple as the sole author of the welfare state, but it is also wrong that he, and the Christian tradition that he represents, should be written out of the script altogether, which has often been his fate at the hands of contemporary writers.

It is fair to say that the welfare state, with its ideal of fairness and the recognition of the worth of each individual regardless of station in life, is the natural offspring of Christian teaching; a society which looks after the poor is a society moulded by a philosophy quite different from naked capitalism. The new welfare state was a tremendous boon for many middle- and working-class families; a health service that could always be accessed, regardless of how much money you had, offered not only healthcare but a blessed freedom from anxiety. Temple's advocacy shows that welfare was entirely congruent with Christian thinking, but it also changed (in ways he could not have foreseen) the Church's relationship with the country.

It is often assumed that before Attlee's reforms there was no help available for the poor but, in fact, this is not so. From the middle of the nineteenth century onwards the UK had one of the Western world's most developed networks of welfare services. It was characterised by voluntary provision, with the mutual and friendly societies delivering a whole range of services. Local authorities and voluntarily run hospitals, together with a national system of 'panel doctors', were financed from health insurance contributions which were set by the state and collected through mutual societies. The Liberal government of 1906 led by Lloyd George introduced a non-contributory and means-tested old age pension for those aged seventy and over.

Within the patchwork of social provision the churches also played an important role supporting many charities with both money and personnel; all denominations, Anglican, Roman Catholic and nonconformist, understood that core to their mission was the relief of want in all its many forms. But what these services could not be was uniform or comprehensive. There were, inevitably, gaps in provision either because of geography or designated status. What Attlee's reforms did was to broaden entitlement and make services nationally available to everybody. But in so doing they robbed the churches of one of their prime purposes and, to put it crudely, one of their main selling points.

With 'the poor' now the responsibility of the state, albeit a Christian state, there was no longer the same need for the churches to involve themselves so much in direct charitable endeavour. That meant that to the upcoming generations after 1945 the churches were no longer demonstrating Christianity in action in quite the same way. As Sam Wells, vicar of St Martin-in-the-Fields puts it, 'seventy years ago the state became the church',[6] and in doing so the Church was, in that sense at least, robbed of some meaning and purpose.

There was another far-reaching consequence of this social revolution which was to align ever more closely the Church of England with left-wing politics; having seen a Labour government enact a raft of legislation bettering the lot of the poor, the Church became the party's ally on many issues. It was in 1917 that a suffragist and preacher, Agnes Maude Royden[7] coined a phrase to describe this association, which has been used ever since – though not always accurately. She said:

---

6   Sam Wells, Russell Rook and David Barclay, *For Good: The Church and the Future of Welfare* (Canterbury Press, 2017).

7   Agnes Royden (1876–1956) was the first woman to become a doctor of divinity and founded the Society for The Ministry of Women in 1929 which campaigned for the ordination of women to the C. of E. priesthood.

The Church [of England] should go forward along the path
of progress and be no longer satisfied only to represent the
Conservative Party at prayer.

That phrase resounded down the decades, and not to the benefit
of the Tories or the Church of England. Royden's words turned
out to be prophetic – the Anglican Church did, indeed, take
the 'path of progress', which has turned out to be a fateful fork
in the road. By the latter decades of the century, certainly from
the 1960s onwards, the Church of England seemed at times,
at least in its pronouncements on social policy, to be a wholly
owned subsidiary of the Labour Party. This was, in fact, more
true of its clergy than its lay worshippers; as recently as 2014
research into the voting intentions of Anglicans showed that
a majority tended to vote Conservative (although 'nominal'
Anglicans – those who rarely or never go to church services
– were majority Labour voting). However, there is a clear and
obvious danger for the Church in becoming so closely identified with the political programme of one party, which is that
it comes to be seen solely as an adjunct, its voice merely one
of the supporting chorus. And what was much more serious
for the Church was that whereas in Temple's case it was the
churchman who could claim to have influenced the politicians,
later and disastrously, roles were reversed.

It was a General Secretary of the Labour Party, Morgan
Phillips, who first quipped that Labour 'owed more to Methodism

than to Marxism', which might well have been true once upon a time, but by the 1960s the influence of the Marxists was in the ascendant. It was natural for the founding generation of Labour people to think in terms of 'building a New Jerusalem'; the party's early history is suffused with an ardour that has echoes of Christian revivalism. But after 1917 the allure of Communism grew ever stronger; why, after all, settle for the gentle gradualism of Christian socialism when you might instead have the big bang of Communist revolution?

Certainly there was a generation of idealistic and militant young people in the '20s and '30s who felt that Britain's democratic tradition would never deliver the social change they demanded, which is why Communism was, for a few decades, both fashionable and influential. The fact that Soviet Communism was also explicitly atheist hastened the decline of Christian influence within Labour. In Archbishop Temple's time, socialism must have seemed a natural bedfellow for the Church; but there clearly should have been a parting of the ways when the Labour Party began to take seriously the idea that politics was a 'class war'. A war between the classes is a profoundly un-Christian notion, antithetical to everything that Christianity teaches.

Within the BBC there has always been natural sympathy for left-wing thinking. Partly this comes from the BBC's ethos of service to the nation which it has interpreted to mean 'inclusivity'. This naturally leads the Corporation to devote much time and effort to illustrating the plight of society's unfortunates. This sympathy also owes something to the fact that the BBC is a 'public corporation', which means it stands somewhat aloof from the capitalist society to which it is home and upon which it reports. The BBC's status as a public corporation leads it to have a kind of fraternal sympathy with the rest of the public sector, and accounts for its occasionally disdainful attitude towards the grubby business of making money.

Thus it was that in the 1960s the BBC turned out to be the most congenial milieu imaginable for a generation of young radicals eager for change. What united them was a commitment to the transgressive. Conventional morality, that is to say the public morality of the 'establishment', was their target and they set about the task of dismantling it with undisguised relish. In serious current affairs programmes they were able to harness the power of television to highlight, often tendentiously, society's problems and discredit the old order; meanwhile, with savage satire on programmes like *That Was The Week That Was*, they mocked the ancient regime. It was a winning formula.

It was the German student revolutionary Rudi Dutschke who coined the phrase the 'long march through the institutions'[8] as a way of achieving revolution from within. Like

---

8   This was Dutschke's interpretation of the work of the Italian Marxist thinker, Antonio Gramsci, which is why the quote is often incorrectly attributed to Gramsci.

other leftist thinkers he thought the sophisticated societies of Western Europe would prove hostile to the kind of Communist revolution imposed on the luckless Russian peasantry in 1917; in bourgeois societies, he reckoned, a more sophisticated approach was needed. And from the '60s onwards a cohort of left-wing politicians, teachers, social workers, lawyers and journalists proved him right. In all these professions young, left-inclined people gained entry and, slowly but surely, ascended through the ranks.

The media was a particular magnet for such people; it doesn't take a genius to work out that if you want to change the world you have to change minds – and there could be no better vehicle for that than the BBC. Highly respected, a bit staid, ubiquitous in the life of the nation, it was ripe for takeover, which is precisely what happened: by the 1990s, through the natural processes of generational change, the whole institution was firmly in the hands of the '60s generation. The infiltration was complete and the radicals were snugly ensconced in the higher echelons of the Corporation, able to ensure that all its output conformed to 'correct' thought. Today, what was once transgressive has become mainstream – though the radicals are never satisfied and are still determined to sweep away what little remains of the old morality. As evidenced, for example, in the BBC's bold and unremitting campaign to achieve the legalisation of euthanasia.

Social conservatives have long complained of bias in the BBC's handling of the topic of assisted dying. In 2010, twenty

MPs signed an Early Day Motion accusing the Corporation of showing 'persistent bias' in favour of euthanasia. The Conservative MP Ann Winterton, who was leader of the group, was supported by four Conservative MPs and one Labour MP in her motion, which stated that the BBC 'have ignored the rights of the disabled, despite the fact that every disability rights group in the UK is opposed to the legalisation of assisted suicide and euthanasia'. In 2013 Dr Peter Saunders wrote to the BBC's Director-General, Lord Tony Hall, saying that the BBC had 'consistently promoted an agenda seeking to change the law on assisted suicide and euthanasia' and had 'given undue prominence to the supporters of this change … while failing to give equal coverage to those who opposed the killing of the terminally ill and disabled'.

Euthanasia is a moral issue of the most serious kind. It cuts to the very heart of how we view life itself. It is a touchstone issue because, aside from any practical consequences a change in the law would have, it has a profound symbolic significance. Once a society decides that certain lives are not worth living and that it is legal to end them, it has set down a fearful marker. It is exactly the kind of issue where the BBC's commitment to full, fair and balanced debate should weigh most heavily, and yet it consistently fails to do so. The BBC has over many years given prominence to heart-wrenching stories of people who want to die. It is not difficult to milk these 'human interest' stories for the purposes of the campaign to allow euthanasia

– that is their whole point. Each of these individual cases is used as a battering ram to persuade public opinion that the only civilised response to these individual tragedies is to allow mercy killing. Where is the counterargument to balance the coverage? The truthful answer is that it has not been heard, and that the well-organised euthanasia campaign gets a free hit time after time. The BBC has enlisted to one side of a deeply controversial argument in a way that flies in the face of its commitment to impartiality.

The typical life cycle of a progressive and transgressive idea like euthanasia goes like this; firstly a pressure group makes the case for change, then a politician takes it up and proposes changing the law. But, before any radical new law can be enacted you first have to soften up public opinion; that's the job of the broadcasters. Carefully selected hard-luck cases are used to enlist the sympathies of the unwary public and, by such means, the revolution progresses. A perfect current example of this process is the debate about cannabis; liberals, who want to see the drug legalised, have seized upon the use of cannabis for medicinal purposes. The drug has therapeutic value in the treatment of some conditions, including epilepsy. The government is under pressure to allow cannabis use in certain circumstances, and this is a demand that, once granted, will bring closer the further step of general legalisation. The beauty of the process is that anyone who opposes the change can be publicly shamed as a heartless reactionary; to know the truth of this, just ask any politician who has tried to speak up for an unfashionable, socially conservative position. Thus, what was transgressive becomes progressive and part of the consensus that coalesces around fashionable opinion; dissent from it risks demonisation at the hands of the media, and ostracism from polite society.

From the 1960s onwards this was the process that conquered and finally vanquished the old morality, with strategic groups of sympathisers in the various professions in league with the broadcasters. Together, in the name of progress, they paved the way for radical new laws which have profoundly changed the standards by which we judge ourselves; some have gained new freedoms as a result, but there have been many others who are victims of the new morality although their stories rarely get told.

It is not possible to point to a precise date when the BBC ceased to uphold traditional Christian morality; there was no signal public moment of apostasy. But as the new morality took shape, at first tentatively, but eventually with overweening confidence, traditional Christian mores were pushed aside. The first act in this drama was set at the Old Bailey in 1960 when the authorities, using the 1959 Obscene Publications Act, prosecuted Penguin Books for publishing D. H. Lawrence's novel *Lady Chatterley's Lover*. The book tells the story of an aristocratic woman who has an affair with her husband's gamekeeper, and its (then provocative) treatment of the class issue, as well as the use of colloquial sexualised language (fuck, cunt, cock etc.), meant that it had been banned from publication in Britain ever since it was written in 1928. The case went before a jury and – sensationally – they acquitted Penguin; it was a decision which, in retrospect, can be seen as firing the starting gun on the revolution which followed. Certainly, in retrospect, it has come to be recognised as a momentous decision which helped define our age. Here is what the prominent liberal QC Geoffrey Robertson wrote in an article in *The Guardian* to mark the fiftieth anniversary of the trial:

> The Old Bailey has, for centuries, provided the ultimate arena for challenging the state. But of all its trials – for murder and mayhem, for treason and sedition – none has had such profound social and political consequences as the trial in 1960 of Penguin Books for publishing *Lady Chatterley's Lover*. The verdict was a crucial step towards the freedom of the written word, at least for works of literary merit (works of no literary merit were not safe until the trial of Oz in 1971, and works of demerit had to await the acquittal of *Inside Linda Lovelace* in 1977) … But the *Chatterley* trial marked the first symbolic moral battle between the humanitarian force of English liberalism and the dead hand of those described by George Orwell as 'the striped-trousered ones who rule', a battle joined in

the 1960s on issues crucial to human rights, including the legalisation of homosexuality and abortion, abolition of the death penalty and of theatre censorship, and reform of the divorce laws. The acquittal of *Lady Chatterley* was the first sign that victory was achievable, and with the guidance of the book's great defender, Gerald Gardiner QC (Labour lord chancellor 1964–70), victory was, in due course, achieved.[9]

The true significance of the trial, as Robertson goes on to explain, lay in the way the jury had overturned a public moral standard inherited from traditional Christian teaching:

> The acquittal was a victory for moral relativism and sexual tolerance, as well as for literary freedom. No other jury verdict in British history has had such a deep social impact … The jury – that iconic representative of democratic society – had given its imprimatur to ending the taboo on sexual discussion in art and entertainment. Within a few years the stifling censorship of the theatre by the lord chamberlain had been abolished, and a gritty realism emerged in British cinema and drama.[10]

---

9 Geoffrey Robertson QC, 'The trial of Lady Chatterley's Lover', *The Guardian*, 22 October 2010.

10 Geoffrey Robertson QC, ibid.

After the Chatterley trial the 'humanitarian forces of English liberalism', as Robertson terms them, entered a long period of uninterrupted success which continues to the present. The battlegrounds he enumerates, divorce, legalisation of homosexuality, abortion, the abolition of the death penalty, had all been areas previously governed by an objective moral standard, laid down by the Christian churches. Moral relativism – that is to say a philosophical stance which claims that nobody is objectively right or wrong – in a sense privatises morality and dictates that we should tolerate the behaviour of others even if we consider it immoral. The abandonment of the idea of an objective morality – that is one that claims there are moral rules that are true and universal which is Lewis's 'natural law' – follows on logically from an atheistic perspective. In a world without God who is to decide 'right' and 'wrong'? The Christian Church's belief that the moral law comes from God – and thus must be obeyed – makes no sense at all to an atheist. Within the BBC, any idea of an objective morality has been jettisoned to be replaced by of a protean morality that is built on the shifting sands of fashionable opinion and is constantly changing its ground.

As for the national church, it rapidly found itself caught up in the painful dilemma of how to come to an accommodation with the emerging new morality. As the moral relativists gained ground, the Church of England found it increasingly difficult to hold the line on traditional Christian teaching. On abortion (an act which the Christian churches believed to be wrong since earliest times) the Anglican Church, while disapproving, allows for exceptions. This is the General Synod's teaching on the matter:

> The Church of England combines strong opposition to abortion with a recognition that there can be – strictly limited – conditions under which it may be morally preferable to any available alternative.

This amounts to saying that abortion is generally wrong, but that it depends on circumstances – an equivocation which avoids the painful business of deciding whether there is, objectively, a right or a wrong. On divorce there is a similar avoidance of absolutes:

> The Church of England teaches that marriage is for life. It also teaches that some marriages, sadly, do fail and, if this should happen, it seeks to be available to all involved. The Church accepts that, in exceptional circumstances, a divorced person may marry again in church during the lifetime of a former spouse.

On homosexuality, the Church has found it impossible to arrive at an agreed position. Liberals within the Church have been campaigning for an open acceptance of homosexual relationships, including gay marriage, but this so far been resisted. In 1998 the Lambeth Conference – which is the gathering of bishops from the worldwide Anglican Communion – came out with the following statement:

> This conference, while rejecting homosexual practice as incompatible with Scripture, calls on all our people to minister pastorally and sensitively to all irrespective of sexual orientation and to condemn irrational fear of homosexuals, violence within marriage and any trivialisation and commercialisation of sex.

But the Lambeth Conference cannot not make binding rulings on doctrine. So the battle within the Church of England has not abated, and the continuing and vigorous campaign by activists for parity of esteem between heterosexual and homosexual relationships has destabilised the Church. The wider Anglican Communion, and particularly the African branches, have expressed firm opposition to relaxing the teaching on homosexuality. The doctrinal formulations on abortion, divorce and homosexuality, doubtless well-meant and compassionate, are carefully attuned to the sensitivities of the age. But they sacrifice moral clarity in their eagerness to allow the get-out clause. The C. of E. has become painfully anxious to be non-judgemental, knowing that to do otherwise is to invite the condemnation of social liberals. And it is in this respect that the role of the BBC matters.

The BBC has wholeheartedly thrown its lot in with the liberal reformers; there has been no 'impartiality' on any of the big moral issues of the past half-century. In every instance, the socially conservative argument has been depicted as callous, reactionary and dogmatic. Any counterargument to the prevailing liberal consensus is now ignored altogether; social conservative voices are conspicuous by their absence on mainstream current affairs programmes. That is sometimes because there is no one in the production teams who understands the social conservative position, so it is no longer considered when programmes are in the making. The liberals now have a national culture moulded by their thinking and their laws; it is their world now – the old morality has been utterly vanquished. So, to take the matter of censorship; it is true that the *Chatterley* trial allowed some literary and artistic works of genuine merit to be made available to us all – a clear gain for society. But in the train of that decision came easy access to uncensored pornography, and as a result, there is now no sexual act that cannot be seen in full graphic detail by a visit to a sex shop or at the touch of a computer keyboard.

Pornography is doubly exploitative: it exploits performers and consumers. So strong is the sex drive that there are many men (and some women) who find it almost impossible to resist. If it is a victory for 'the humanitarian forces of English liberalism' that all now have access to pornography, is that a wholly beneficial outcome? Is pornography, in other words, a benefit to society? Here is what the American College of Pediatricians had to say on the matter in 2016:

> The availability and use of pornography has become almost ubiquitous among adults and adolescents. Consumption of pornography is associated with many negative emotional, psychological, and physical health outcomes. These include increased rates of depression, anxiety, acting out and violent behaviour, younger age of sexual debut, sexual promiscuity, increased risk of teen pregnancy, and a distorted view of relationships between men and women. For adults, pornography results in an increased likelihood of divorce which is also harmful to children. The American College of Pediatricians urges healthcare professionals to communicate the risks of pornography use to patients and their families and to offer resources both to protect children from viewing pornography and to treat individuals suffering from its negative effects.[11]

This is a surprisingly unequivocal statement which admits to no uncertainty on the matter. The representative body of those American doctors who devote their professional lives to the care of children have come to a strikingly clear-cut view of the matter: pornography is harmful. It is true that other

---

11 American College of Pediatricians website, June 2016.

similar bodies – like our own Royal College of Paediatricians and Child Health – have been much more reticent and seem to have no official view at all. Could this be ascribed to simple moral cowardice, reflecting a reluctance by the college to involve itself in public controversy?

In any event, it is surely the case that a strong argument can, and should, be made for censoring pornography, but it is not one that you will hear promoted on the BBC, or indeed anywhere else in the mainstream British media. And that raises the question 'why not?' After all, we have now had decades of more or less unrestricted access to pornography and there is much evidence that it is harmful to children and adults. The reason for the deafening silence is that social liberalism has now achieved an intellectual hegemony among media professionals as it has in both the law and education. It seems that there must not be a debate on this matter, because to do so would be to challenge something, which, in the view of prominent liberals like Geoffrey Robertson, underpins the whole edifice of social liberalism. Perhaps if we started to question the wisdom of permitting pornography, other assumptions which are foundational to the new liberal order might also unravel?

Take next the question of divorce. There is a huge amount of academic research into the effects of divorce, and in particular, its effects on children. This is not the place to attempt any sort of comprehensive review of the literature, but what is striking to the lay reader who takes the trouble to have a look at what researchers have discovered, is that there are almost no studies which suggest divorce is beneficial for children. The balance of opinion among those researchers who have examined the question is overwhelmingly that it is a very negative influence on the lives of children. Here is a representative conclusion – one of many that could be cited – this one from the *Linacre Quarterly* published by the US National Library of Medicine, National Institutes of Health:

> Nearly three decades of research evaluating the impact of family structure on the health and well-being of children demonstrates that children living with their married, bio-logical parents consistently have better physical, emotional, and academic well-being. Pediatricians and society should promote the family structure that has the best chance of producing healthy children. The best scientific literature to date suggests that, with the exception of parents faced with unresolvable marital violence, children fare better when parents work at maintaining the marriage. Con-sequently, society should make every effort to support healthy marriages and to discourage married couples from divorcing.[12]

---

12 *Linacre Quarterly*, November 2014; 81(4): pp. 378–387.

Anyone who starts looking at the academic literature on divorce soon finds that there is a common storyline: compared with the children of married couples, the children of divorced parents suffer higher levels of anxiety, worse overall mental health, lower academic attainment, difficulties forming stable relationships, higher levels of addiction and substance abuse, higher levels of obesity and even a higher incidence of many other physical conditions. One study from Sweden, which has data extending back over a century, showed that, having allowed for other variables, the children who go through divorce have higher eventual mortality i.e. they die younger. Divorce, in a word, is a poisonous cocktail of ills for children. And in Britain the number of divorces has soared since no-fault divorce was introduced in 1969; whereas in 1968 there were 45,000 divorces in England and Wales, by 1993 the figure had nearly quadrupled to 165,000.

What is just as significant is that, over roughly the same period, the number of marriages sharply declined – from 404,000 in 1971 to 247,000 in 2014. This figure also spells trouble because extensive research in the US and Europe has demonstrated that cohabitation is an inherently unstable arrangement. And the effects on children when cohabiting parents split up are very similar to the fallout from divorce. According to the Marriage Foundation:

> Three in five (62 per cent) British children born to unmarried parents living together experience family breakdown

before they hit their teens. In contrast, only 45 per cent of American children, 15 per cent of Belgian children and six per cent of Spanish children born to cohabiting parents undergo the same seismic shift in their family dynamic by the age of 12. Almost without exception across the world, cohabiting couples are more unstable than married couples, even when they have children. In the UK, children born to cohabiting parents are 94 per cent more likely to see their parents break up before age twelve, compared to children born to married parents. Even among married couples, the UK has some of the highest rates of family breakdown in Europe. A third (32 per cent) of British twelve year olds whose parents were married when they were born have experienced family breakdown. In Austria the figure is nine per cent and in France eleven per cent.[13]

According to Geoffrey Robertson, as quoted above, in the 1960s divorce fell into that category of liberal causes that were crucial to the attainment of 'human rights'. But it was the *Chatterley* decision, as he sees it, that opened the way for other liberal reforms like the 1969 Divorce Reform Act. And today we can see the consequence of that reform – a country

---

13 Marriage Foundation February 2017. The MF was started by High Court Judge in the Family Division, Sir Paul Coleridge in 2012. It works to prevent what it calls the 'scourge' of family breakdown in the UK.

where the needs of children are subordinate to the desires of their parents and where, as a result, millions have had their happiness destroyed and their life chances damaged. There is a studied lack of interest at the BBC and other media in this phenomenon; and it is not only the media which is apparently unconcerned. The most senior family judge in England and Wales, Sir James Munby, said during a speech at Liverpool University in May 2018 that 'In contemporary Britain the family takes an almost infinite variety of forms.' He went on:

> Children live in households where their parents may be married or unmarried. They may be brought up by a single parent, by two parents or even by three parents. Their parents may or may not be their natural parents … Many adults and children, whether through choice or circumstance, live in families more or less removed from what, until comparatively recently, would have been recognised as the typical nuclear family. This, I stress, is not merely the reality; it is, I believe, a reality which we should welcome and applaud.

It is all much of a muchness, apparently, to the learned Sir James, whether or not traditional families survive in modern Britain. For a senior judge to be so cavalier in his attitude towards the family, the most important human institution in every society now and throughout human history, beggars belief. It was striking that the BBC ignored his speech – there was no big interview with Sir James on *Today* or any of the other main news programmes; clearly what he had to say was neither, in the BBC's view, shocking nor new. But what if Sir James had taken the opposite tack? Suppose he had spoken up for traditional families and cautioned against informal family structures because of their proven disadvantages as child-rearing environments? Then we can be sure the BBC would have leapt on his words, outraged that anyone should have the temerity to challenge the current, permissive consensus. And while Sir James is merrily applauding and welcoming the demise of the old, despised, nuclear family, the statistics about the welfare of children continue to paint a grim picture. In a 2016 international comparison of how children rated their sense of wellbeing, and specifically, how they felt about their life satisfaction, England came near the bottom of the table – thirteenth out of sixteen. Jonathan Bradshaw, professor of social policy at the University of York, who co-edited the report, was shocked by the findings. He said:

> You will see that we come bottom of the league table on quite a lot of things – very unhappy with the way you look and your own body; relationships with teachers are poor; dissatisfaction with school performance; dissatisfaction

with the area in which you live; quite dissatisfied with family life, although not so much the people you live with and the house you live in.[14]

It would be reasonable, would it not, to make some link perhaps between family breakdown and the unhappiness of the nation's children? But this is a debate studiously avoided by the BBC because, if it were pursued, it would ineluctably lead to the conclusion that we should do more to encourage marriage and stable families. Such a conclusion runs counter to the liberal consensus assembled since the 1960s in the wake of the *Chatterley* trial. Liberal social policies, like those pursued in Britain for the past half-century, come with a high price tag – and the people who have paid it are the nation's children.

There is no particular mystery about what has happened, or why: the abandonment of an objective moral order is a consequence of the triumph of atheistic thought. Nowhere is that triumph more obvious, or more complete, than within the media and in the BBC especially. Whereas in the 1940s when the BBC felt able, unapologetically, to broadcast the words of C. S. Lewis, sixty years later it was the works of another Oxford man, Richard Dawkins, who it took to its heart. In 2006

---

14 Damien Gayle, 'Children in England near bottom in international happiness table', *The Guardian*, 2016.

Professor Dawkins published *The God Delusion* which purported to debunk religion and to convert people from what he believes is an irrational belief in a supernatural being. In place of religious belief, he says, there will be rationalism and, through the endeavours of scientists, eventually mankind will be delivered from the shackles of, what he would call, superstition.

The BBC attached enormous importance to this book and its author was repeatedly, and respectfully, interviewed on all the main BBC outlets on radio and television. The BBC reacted as though Professor Dawkins, a geneticist, really had nailed the essence of the argument and settled the matter once and for all. And yet, a decade or more later, his book looks like just another contribution to the debate – neither definitive nor profound. Dawkins is a leading exponent of 'scientism', which is the ideology of science that teaches that science can explain everything, and by extension, solve all our problems. Without God in the equation this naturally raises the question: how should we live in this new rational world? Helpfully, in *The God Delusion*, Professor Dawkins gives us his answer with alternatives to the biblical Ten Commandments:

1. Do not do to others what you would not want them to do to you.
2. In all things, strive to cause no harm.
3. Treat your fellow human beings, your fellow living things,

and the world in general with love, honesty, faithfulness and respect.

4. Do not overlook evil or shrink from administering justice, but always be ready to forgive wrongdoing freely admitted and honestly regretted.

5. Live life with a sense of joy and wonder.

6. Always seek to be learning something new.

7. Test all things; always check your ideas against the facts, and be ready to discard even a cherished belief if it does not conform to them.

8. Never seek to censor or cut yourself off from dissent; always respect the right of others to disagree with you.

9. Form independent opinions on the basis of your own reason and experience; do not allow yourself to be led blindly by others.

10. Question everything.

According to Professor Dawkins this list is one that any 'ordinary, decent person' should subscribe to. He also adds a few extra injunctions on how to live:

1. Enjoy your own sex life (so long as it damages nobody else) and leave others to enjoy theirs in private whatever their inclinations, which are none of your business.

2. Do not discriminate or oppress on the basis of sex, race or (as far as possible) species.

3. Do not indoctrinate your children. Teach them how to think for themselves, how to evaluate evidence, and how to disagree with you.
4. Value the future on a timescale longer than your own.

Most of this is intellectual pap – all that's lacking, one feels, is an injunction to 'travel the world' and work for world peace – but aside from the fatuity of the exercise, to what extent does it cohere as a workable philosophy of life? Take, for instance, the instruction to 'enjoy your own sex life', and now try to reconcile it with No. 2 on the list 'strive to do no harm'. 'Enjoying one's own sex life' sounds very much like an invitation to go where your sex drive leads you; this, for many people, will rule out 'faithfulness' (No. 3 on the list) and would likely prove an obstacle to stable marriage or cohabitation. And, very probably, the divorces and separations that will result from heedlessly 'enjoying one's own sex life' will hurt and damage any children involved. Professor Dawkins, it should be noted, has been divorced three times.

The significance of *The God Delusion* lay in the way in which it was promoted by the BBC. The book was treated with reverence, and the lavish coverage helped to propel its author to the highest pinnacle of intellectual celebrity. He is now one of that small, glittering band of international intellectual superstars in demand around the world. The BBC was not his only promoter – *The Times*, *The Guardian* and *The Independent*, as well as most other serious television and media outlets, all paid homage to the new guru – but the BBC's imprimatur is always worth more than the others. The Corporation still commands respect among media professionals; there is a noticeable cultural cringe when other broadcasters, particularly those from places like Australia and Canada, come into contact with it. Partly thanks to the BBC's heady sponsorship, *The God Delusion* became a global phenomenon which – given its intellectual mediocrity – takes some explaining. The eminent American sociologist Peter Berger[15] gave much thought to the general phenomenon of secularisation, and his observations are peculiarly apt as a way of explaining the success of Dawkins's book:

> There exists an international subculture composed of people with Western-type higher education, especially in the humanities and social sciences, that is indeed secularized. This subculture is the principal 'carrier' of progressive, Enlightened beliefs and values. While its members are relatively thin on the ground, they are very influential, as they control the institutions that provide the 'official' definitions of reality, notably the educational system, the media of mass communication, and the higher reaches of the legal system.

---

15 Peter Ludwig Berger (1929–2017) was an Austrian-born American protestant theologian and sociologist.

> They are remarkably similar all over the world today, as they
> have been for a long time … I may observe in passing that
> the plausibility of secularization theory owes much to this
> international subculture.[16]

So ubiquitous was the coverage that it felt at the time as if *The God Delusion* was being promoted as a quasi-official philosophy; away with the Book of Common Prayer, in with a book for the common man. And in the context of Berger's 'subculture', *The God Delusion* has become one of the standard texts of the secularists; an enormously influential work colouring the opinions of millions of people around the world. The fact of its essential vacuity doesn't matter because, with its reputation enormously inflated by an uncritical media, it has been promoted to the status of holy writ.

The old moral code is difficult to live up to; its stern injunctions run counter to human instinct in every respect. It calls for self-restraint and self-abnegation and does so in the name of a higher power. That's why people find it difficult, and why many don't like it. Mr Dawkins's new commandments have the great advantage of not being at all irksome – they are, in fact, a very agreeable and flexible set of rules which allow an individual to do pretty much what they want. They certainly

---

16 Peter Ludwig Berger, *The De-secularisation of the World* (William B. Eerdmans Publishing, 1999), p. 10.

would not act as a brake on selfish impulses. The crucial point to grasp is that because they admit to no outside authority, but depend entirely on the individual's own judgement (one might say 'conscience') of what is right and what is wrong, they validate an infinite variety of outcomes. Each man becomes his own 'god', and sets the rules accordingly. The obvious problem is that most people find it difficult to resist the temptation to self-justify their actions, and tend to give themselves the benefit of the doubt.

The noble lie at the heart of this new morality is that we can, as individuals and as a society, dispense with an objective moral code without harmful consequences. The claim is that the old moral code was judgemental and harsh and based on a non-existent Deity who had supposedly laid down rules about human conduct; in fact, say the atheists, the rules were concocted by power hungry priests. The new moral code, they say, which dispenses with God altogether, allows everyone to live happier lives – free from the guilt that the traditional rules engendered. This idea has been successfully marketed to the country (after all, it's not that difficult to persuade people to do what their instincts urge them to do) and, exercising our democratic free will, we have enshrined in law measures that overturn the old moral code.

The new dispensation has had profound consequences, not least on the nation's mental health. Increasing incidence of mental illness has been apparent in recent years, not surprisingly because the UK has one of the highest rates of mental health problems in the world. According to an NHS survey reported in 2017, at any one time, a sixth of the population is suffering from a mental health problem. As reported by the BBC website: 'It seems to be getting more common – or at least among those with severe symptoms. While the proportion of people affected does not appear to have risen in the past few years, if you go back a little further there has certainly been a steady increase.'[17]

The result of our national, transgressive moral revolution is now apparent: a horribly diminished sense of security for millions of children and a coarsening and debasement of our attitudes to sex, plus a rise in mental illness across the population. In addition, there has been a profound change in the value we put on human life itself. It is often said that contemporary Britain is a post-Christian country; if so, the ills which afflict the nation today cannot be laid at the door of the old belief system. This country of unhappy children and uncertain adults – this is the world social liberal values have conjured into being.

The BBC which, once upon a time, understood its responsibilities differently and promoted a straightforward Christian view of the world, has been the midwife to this transformation; in fact, more than the midwife – an active agent of change

---

17 See: http://www.bbc.co.uk/news/health-41125009

agitating for the new morality. And, the change having been successfully realised – with permissive liberal values now triumphant – the BBC no longer even allows a social conservative challenge to the new dispensation. Any claim by the Corporation, to be 'impartial' in this debate is a lie.

CHAPTER SIX

AUNTIE: SHE'S ONE OF THE SISTERHOOD

EXACTLY WHY THE BBC came to be known as 'Auntie' seems lost in time, but according to the BBC itself the nickname arose sometime in the 1950s. The comedian and presenter Kenny Everett[1] is credited by some with popularising the soubriquet, but there are other more fanciful explanations, among them, for instance, that it derives from the Romany word for auntie which is 'bibi' – which seems pretty unlikely. Whatever the exact provenance of the 'Auntie' tag, it was once in common and affectionate usage; it conjured up the image of

---

1 Kenny Everett (1944–1995) was a comedian, television presenter and radio DJ who mainly worked for the BBC and enjoyed huge popular success.

the BBC as a conventional, rather conservative middle-aged woman, somewhat disapproving at times, but commonsensical and always certain that she was acting in our best interests. Auntie was also, very clearly, middle-class; she was the kind of woman who didn't like vulgarity and put great store by keeping up standards in a rather traditional kind of way. You don't hear the Auntie tag used so often these days; it doesn't seem quite so appropriate now that Auntie has transformed herself from a rather prim guardian of middle-class rectitude into a feminist warrior. After all, traditional aunties always had a traditional morality – what they never, ever had was an ideology.

Feminism is now core to the BBC's belief system. And, while once upon a time, feminists had something worth fighting for (equality in the broadest sense), now that has been achieved, feminism has morphed into a much broader political campaign which aims to conquer new territory. In doing so it has become divisive; the single most important thing to understand about contemporary feminism is that it is a movement, held together by an inconsistent philosophy, which has no capacity to bring men and women together: it divides, rather than unites. By insisting on continuing the fight when the original enemy (men and their assumed superiority) have conceded the argument, British feminists are, metaphorically, slaying opponents who have already surrendered. They are bayoneting the wounded. The effect of this is to poison further relations between the sexes.

At the heart of modern feminism is the demand for equality between the sexes. In this context, equality means the state of being equal, especially in regard to rights or opportunities; implicit in the campaign for equality has been the need for legislation to achieve it. But equality, importantly, is not synonymous with fairness. Equality is to fairness what legalism is to justice: fairness and justice are the things, above all, that we want – equality and legalism are merely possible routes to achieving them, but neither guarantee the ends we desire. The essence of fairness is not that everyone gets the same (although in some circumstances it might be), it is that every individual gets what they need. Fairness is always the prerequisite of a just society, and unfairness should never go unchallenged – but inequality can sometimes be justified. And whereas equality can be legislated into existence, fairness, like justice, cannot be mandated by law – it is too subtle a quality for that. Unfortunately, modern feminism has become obsessed by the demand for equality – sometimes at the expense of fairness. There is a fundamental confusion about this. The Equality and Human Rights Commission, the body set up by the Blair government in 2007 to oversee the equality revolution, sets out a useful definition of its own primary purpose:

> Equality is about ensuring that every individual has an equal opportunity to make the most of their lives and talents. It is also the belief that no one should have poorer

life chances because of the way they were born, where they come from, what they believe, or whether they have a disability. Equality recognises that historically certain groups of people with protected characteristics such as race, disability, sex and sexual orientation have experienced discrimination.[2]

This is a very noble definition, but there is nothing in it, I believe, which a good person should take exception to. But when the EHRC goes on to explain the campaign for equal pay – a prime objective of British feminists – it had this to say about the current state of affairs:

> However, many aspects of British life are still not fair. For example:
> - Women still earn significantly less than men for every hour they work.
> - In 2007, 97 per cent of hairdressing apprentices were women, receiving on average £109 per week, and 98 per cent of engineering apprentices were male, receiving on average £189 per week.[3]

---

2   Equality and Human Rights Commission website, May 2018, see: https://www.equalityhumanrights.com/en/secondary-education-resources/useful-information/understanding-equality

3   This was also originally from the Equality and Human Rights Commission website, but has since been deleted.

This is, frankly, unintelligent on a number of levels. How is it 'not fair' that hairdressing apprentices should be lower paid than engineering apprentices? Presumably hairdressers pay their trainees a rate their businesses can afford; if all hairdressers were forced to pay their trainees the extra £80 per week how could the money be found? Either by putting up the price of a haircut to customers or by reducing the profits of the hairdresser. Is either of those outcomes 'fair'? Not necessarily so – they might, in fact, be very unfair both to customers and to the owners of hairdressing salons. Neither is the fact that many women go into hairdressing while few go into engineering evidence of 'unfairness'. There are many reasons why males and females differ in their occupational choices, and despite the fact that the professions themselves nowadays go to great lengths to ensure that they are equally open to both sexes, it is very unlikely that engineering (or hairdressing) will ever achieve a 50/50 ratio.

The slogan 'equal pay for equal work' has a pleasing simplicity, but it makes a better debating point than a policy prescription. There are many circumstances where work might appear equal and yet a pay differential is logical. Take, for instance, footballers; there are professional players of both sexes – should they earn equal pay? Clearly they don't, because the men's game generates huge revenues while the women's game doesn't. But in an obvious sense they do the same 'work'. The slogan can only translate into reality where work is obviously and genuinely 'equal', and therein lies the problem.

The BBC itself became very exercised about the issue when it was discovered that its female presenters were often paid less than males working on the same programme. But those same figures also showed that some males were paid much more than other males; but the fees paid to these individuals, both male and female, were partly dependent on factors such as experience and performance. It is not necessarily fair to pay all the presenters on a programme the same money; to do so might achieve 'equality', but it might also be unfair. However, the crude measure the BBC adopts when debating the issue means that all nuance is lost. The primitive egalitarianism of contemporary feminism has infused the BBC's entire output in a way that is unhealthy and inhibits free debate.

The original feminists had a just cause: they wanted to be treated equally under the law; they wanted to have their intelligence and talents valued as equal to those of men; they wanted to participate fully in the life of the nations they inhabited and they wanted their dignity as women recognised and enhanced. They demanded that the law should not discriminate against women, and the organised fight to achieve these aims began early in the nineteenth century. Some historians of feminism are keen on the idea of dividing the movement into 'waves', an approach that has the advantage of dividing a sprawling subject into bite-sized chunks. In this framework the first wave feminists were the women suffragettes and their male supporters who, from the mid-nineteenth century onwards, began achieving legislative change enabling women to vote. It was a piecemeal process which saw change come in fits and starts but, eventually, votes for women was recognised as the natural and fair outcome for democratic nations.

It wasn't a wholly Anglo-centric process, but it is fair to say that debate about female suffrage was most vigorously contested in countries of the English-speaking world, and it is New Zealand which holds the proud distinction of being the first country to enfranchise women in 1893. By the middle of the twentieth century nearly every country with any pretensions to modernity had given women the vote; a landmark came in 1950 when India, the world's biggest democracy, did so. There were laggards, some of them surprising – Switzerland only came on board in 1971 – some of them less so – Saudi Arabia finally flirted with modernity in 2011 by allowing some women to vote in some municipal elections.

Today female suffrage is near enough universal – although, of course, there are still countries where few women vote and others where there are no votes (at least meaningful ones) for either men or women. So it is fair to say that now, in the twenty-first century, the first, and arguably the most important goal of the feminist movement, has been achieved: votes for women is now seen as normal in any functioning democracy. But vanguard feminists were quick to argue that votes for women was the beginning, not the end of the campaign. Now they had the vote, they argued that there were many changes, in expectations, in attitudes and in societal structures, needed in order to achieve equality between the sexes.

The so-called 'second wave' feminists came to prominence in the 1960s determined to dismantle obstacles to female advancement. The writer Betty Friedan, whose book *The Feminine Mystique* sold three million copies in three years, gave modern feminists a foundational text which talked of 'the problem that has no name'. Meanwhile, in the UK, gifted polemicists like Germaine Greer forced women's issues to the forefront of public debate and politicians like Barbara Castle showed that women could achieve real power in the hitherto masculine-dominated world of politics. New laws were enacted which overturned restrictions previously placed on women: the Abortion Act 1967 which made abortion available on demand; the Divorce Act of 1969 which introduced no-fault divorce; the Equal Pay Act of 1970 and the Sex Discrimination Act of 1975 which made discrimination on the grounds of gender illegal in most instances. The legislative drive for equality under the law culminated in 2010 with the Equality Act which brought provisions from 116 separate pieces of legislation under one legal roof. Each of these new laws marked another milestone in the long journey to enshrine female equality under the law.[4]

---

4 Many of these laws also aimed to improve the lot of other groups – the disabled, ethnic minorities etc. – and the Equality Act is not solely about women, but the driving force behind much of the legislation was the feminist agenda.

By the late 1970s the feminist movement looked unstoppable; the tide of opinion was on their side, legislative battles had been fought and won and, to that extent, hostilities might have been expected to lessen. But, in fact, feminism moved into a more combative stance, paradoxically just as the UK got its first female Prime Minister. The reason for feminism's success was the underlying justice of their cause; men of my generation (born in the 1950s) put up little resistance to the feminist case because, in essence, we had heard all the arguments and decided that the feminists were right. Parliament – then as now dominated by males – passed one law after another enhancing and protecting the rights of women; so much for the oppressive patriarchy of feminist imaginings! If there really had been a patriarchy determined to thwart female empowerment, it was singularly useless at defending male prerogatives.

Third wave feminism arrived sometime in the 1990s – although, as ever in these matters, there is heated debate among participants about when it first became visible and what, if anything, distinguishes the third from the second wave. There is, however, some measure of agreement that the theory of 'intersectionality', originated by the black American feminist and lawyer Kimberlé Williams Crenshaw in 1989 is central to it.[5] Intersectionality theory teaches that there is

---

5   Kimberlé Williams Crenshaw (b. 1959) is an American civil rights advocate and scholar of critical race theory. She is a full-time professor at the UCLA School of Law, where she specialises in gender and race.

an 'interlocking matrix of oppression', which affects groups because of their class, race, sexual orientation, age, disability or gender. It is thus a way of uniting many disparate groups in a single narrative; intersectionality allows anyone to march under the umbrella of feminism as long as they can lay claim to some kind of oppression, and it has become standard fare among mainstream feminists. Here is what Kristin Aune, a feminist author and fellow at the Centre for Trust, Peace and Social Relations at Coventry University has to say about contemporary feminism:

> Today's feminist movement is more diverse than ever before. Feminism has become more attentive to the wider range of experiences of those oppressed by gender norms and stereotypes, including men, non-binary and trans people.[6]

In practice, it turns out not to be so simple to unite different kinds of supposed injustice in one popular front, as the bitter argument within feminism around the 'trans' question demonstrates. When the trans lobby first gathered steam in the 1990s, most feminists seemed well disposed towards transgendered people – that is, people who suffer from what is technically called 'gender dysphoria', which is the state of anxiety and

---

6   Kristin Aune, 'Why feminism still matters to young people', The Conversation, 6 February 2018.

distress caused by a mismatch between biological sex and gender identity. So you might be a 'man' trapped in a female body or a 'woman' condemned to live with all the physical appurtenances of the male sex. Perhaps, at first, this didn't seem problematic to feminists, because gender dysphoria is a rare condition, and anyway, feminists might well have reasoned that there was little to fear from men who wanted to 'live as women'. According to clinicians who have studied gender identity disorder (GID), the condition affects between 0.05 per cent (1 in 2,000) and 1.2 per cent (more than 1 in 100).[7] But in recent years the number of men identifying as female has risen sharply, which has sparked a sharp backlash from second wave feminists like Germaine Greer who bluntly remarked:

> Just because you lop off your dick and then wear a dress doesn't make you a fucking woman. I've asked my doctor to give me long ears and liver spots and I'm going to wear a brown coat but that won't turn me into a fucking cocker spaniel.[8]

---

7 These figures need to be handled carefully, because they don't always compare like for like; the low figure above is for adults in the Netherlands and Belgium, while the high figure is for New Zealand teenagers. And these guesses of how many people might be suffering from the condition. When it gets down to estimating how many people would actually be diagnosed as having GID according to current clinical criteria, the figures are actually much lower.

8 Germaine Greer, comments on *Newsnight*, 23 October 2015.

The ire of feminists like Greer was partly due to their chagrin at seeing the rights they struggled to win being appropriated by people whose claim to be female might be considered, at the very least, debatable. Trans women raise a host of practical problems too; should someone 'self-identifying' as a woman be allowed into traditionally women-only spaces like lavatories and changing rooms, even if they have a penis? And should they be allowed to compete against cisgender women in sporting contests? There are no definitive statistics on numbers, but nearly all researchers seem to agree that there are more male to female transitions (MTF) than female to male (FTM); MTF seem to outnumber FTM by at least 3:1 and some studies put the ratio much higher. As to why this should be so there are any number of theories and here's my own based on nothing but gut instinct: it is the case that in developed countries the feminist movement has been the 'winning side' in recent decades and with that backdrop it is perhaps not surprising that it has become more attractive to transition to become female. Under the impact of massive publicity it has become fashionable for de-masculinised men to switch gender, and so, there has been an increase in numbers; also, FTM transition has always been less difficult and less noticeable, so the ratios quoted might be intrinsically skewed towards MTF.

Greer's comments made her the target for much abuse: she was labelled a TERF (a trans exclusionary radical feminist) and she was barred from speaking at some events. The *Newsnight* interview was a rare example of allowing an argument based on robust common sense to be aired, and Greer's status as an icon of the feminist movement is the only reason why she was given that platform: the generality of BBC output on the debate has been much more accommodating to the 'trans' viewpoint.

Indeed, from the moment the debate went mainstream (for which the BBC can take much credit), the Corporation has taken the claims of the transgendered pretty much at face value. This is very much in line with third wave feminist 'intersectional' dogma; all victim groups speak the language of 'rights' – as did the feminists themselves – therefore, any group that can portray itself as discriminated against, and can establish this in general public discourse, must, under the terms of 'intersectionality', be given support by the feminist mainstream. This makes it impossible for the BBC to challenge the claims of any group that has taken on feminism's imprimatur, because the BBC itself is so wholly signed-up to the feminist agenda.[9]

This is not to say that the BBC – or indeed the rest of us – should not be sympathetic to the awful plight of that tiny minority who do suffer from GID; confusion around a

---

9   The start of transgender campaign can be roughly dated to 1992 when Leslie Feinberg wrote a pamphlet entitled 'Transgender Liberation: a movement whose time has come'. She called on the trans community to compose its own linguistic definitions as a way of countering alleged oppression.

fundamental aspect of the self, like gender, must be a heavy cross to bear. But the BBC, faithful to the creed of intersectionality, has made the notion of changing one's gender seem almost commonplace. The claims of those who say they speak for the transgendered 'community' go unchallenged, while the obvious practical problems are overlooked. Therefore, little was made of the participation of 'trans' athletes at the Commonwealth Games in Australia in the spring of 2018. One of them, a weightlifter called Laurel Hubbard, who was born male, 'transitioned' in her thirties and now competes as a woman. In her first event as a woman she lifted 17kg more than her nearest rival – a winning margin that suggests her success had much to do with her original biological make-up.

This kind of absurdity – aided and abetted by the BBC's embarrassed silence on the issue – has the potential to make a mockery of female sporting contests. It will not be long before a trans athlete demands entry to a major competition – Wimbledon, for instance – where the prize money available (currently £2.25 million for the Ladies' singles champion) is a very considerable inducement to 'becoming female'. Conforming to the dictates of current progressive thinking on transgenderism will make public criticism nearly impossible; as for cisgender females, they will have to lump it – that's part of the price you pay for 'intersectionality'.

The BBC's complacency about the 'trans' movement is also deeply unfair to the country's adolescents who – along with all the traditional problems associated with that age group – must now navigate waters in which, bizarrely, gender has become elective – a matter of choice, seemingly regardless of biology. This 'gender theory', once the preserve of a radical fringe, has now seeped into the mainstream; in fact, it's worse than that, it is the assumed starting point for discussion of the issue. For BBC interviewers to do otherwise would be to risk being 'judgemental' about an issue which intersectionality deems a progressive cause under the protective umbrella of feminism; which is why the BBC is unable to confront this cruel madness head-on.

While transgender rights are the latest battleground, it was the campaign first to legalise abortion then to consolidate and defend abortion rights that was always of paramount importance to the feminists of the 1960s. In winning that battle they laid the foundations of their future successes. The cadre of feminist women in the vanguard of the movement who gained their campaigning spurs in the abortion debate were thereafter battle-hardened. A strong, well-organised, well-funded and politically savvy campaigning movement was born, and in the succeeding half-century it has not tasted defeat. British feminists have tenaciously defended Britain's abortion industry, putting any criticism of the clinics and practitioners out of bounds for the BBC and most of the rest of the mainstream media. Abortion is absolutely central to modern feminism; free access to abortion can be said to be a

foundational doctrine of the entire modern feminist movement. No other tenet of the creed is defended so stoutly, and
yet it remains an issue where even the combined efforts of the
feminist movement, the BBC and other media outlets has not
been able fully to dispel the sense of moral unease that still
clings to the whole abortion question. That this is the case is
unsurprising; abortion has never been universally accepted –
even by those who call themselves feminists – and there is a
long record of distinguished women who opposed it.

Some of the feminist pioneers of the nineteenth century,
women like Susan B. Anthony and Alice Paul, considered
abortion to be the worst kind of exploitation of women and,
in general, the early feminist movement was against abortion;
but you will listen in vain for any echo of these ideas in the
contemporary British feminist discourse. This isn't because all
British feminists are of one mind in approving abortion, but
rather because the voices of pro-life feminists are screened out.
In fact, there are some in the feminist movement who argue
that a woman cannot be truly feminist unless she supports
abortion on demand. In America, where the debate about
abortion is still vigorously contested, there is an anti-abortion
feminist organisation, Feminists for Life; in Britain, thanks in
large part to the BBC's stance on the issue, the abortion debate
is virtually moribund. And yet, doubts still remain.

It is easy to understand why there should be lingering
moral qualms about abortion; a foetus in the womb is a living

being, as everyone must surely know in their heart. Of course, until a certain point of development, the foetus cannot have an independent existence. But every foetus, unless destined for spontaneous abortion (miscarriage) has the potential to become a human being; arguments which deny the humanity of the foetus on the grounds of non-viability are specious. So-called 'late-term' abortions – where the foetus is well-developed – do not arouse misgivings because, on some magic day during the nine months, the foetus suddenly becomes 'human'; they arouse misgivings because the longer the pregnancy has gone on the more difficult it is to ignore the humanity of the baby in the womb. The cold utilitarianism of the pro-abortionists ('this child is inconvenient, therefore it can be disposed of') runs counter to the deepest feelings of human beings.

How and why 'abortion rights' became so central to the feminist cause has much to do with the way in which militant feminists have argued the issue from the perspective of 'a woman's right to choose'. This elevates the individual woman's 'agency' – that is, her right to autonomous decision-making – above every other consideration. In this argument nothing can be allowed which curtails, restricts or impedes this freedom; it is an absolutist position. Investing all females with this power of life and death – albeit in respect only of their own children – runs counter to the way society has moved on the issue, as it pertains to all other groups, male and female. On the question of capital punishment, for instance, European societies have moved firmly in the 'pro-life' position. But feminism credits womankind with a special – and superior – ability to make these choices unfettered by any moral considerations.

Women, feminists say, must go unchallenged in this area, simply by virtue of being women and whatever they decide is beyond the reproach of others. This is why any male intervention in this debate is decried by feminists: 'It's not your decision', they say. But abortion cannot be lifted out of the moral arena by the diktat of feminists; it cannot be ring-fenced and made a matter only for women to decide. The historical record shows that all societies have taken an interest in the matter of abortion, precisely because the fate of the next generation can never be a matter of indifference to any community.

It is striking that all the world's main religious traditions have, generally speaking, disapproved of abortion; here for instance is John Calvin enunciating a stern Christian doctrine on the matter:

> The unborn, though enclosed in the womb of his mother, is already a human being, and it is an almost monstrous crime to rob it of life which it has not yet begun to enjoy. If it seems more horrible to kill a man in his own house than in a field, because a man's house is his most secure place of refuge, it ought surely to be deemed more atrocious

to destroy the unborn in the womb before it has come
to light.

In Judaism, Hinduism, Islam and Buddhism there are ancient
texts and references which condemn abortion. This is not
to argue that abortion was never practised or sometimes
tolerated in these communities: there have always been circumstances where deliberately aborting a child was seen as
sometimes necessary, even if undesirable. What religions
teach on the issue can, of course, be dismissed by unbelievers:
'What is that to me?', they might well argue. But the world's
great religions are repositories of communal wisdom acquired
through the centuries; what they teach is the distillation of
generations of profound contemplation about life itself. Each
religion differs from the others in important ways, but the
fact that on abortion they all arrive at more or less the same
position should surely give pause for thought. It is the height
of arrogance to assume that these insights can be dispensed
with by our own generation, and that this wisdom has been
superseded by feminist doctrine.

The final chapter on the abortion debate in the UK has
yet to be written – despite the current unchallenged status of
hard-line feminist dogma. There is a fatal flaw in the feminist
argument on abortion which concerns the matter of human
rights. The feminist movement itself is built on the demand
for rights – it was in pursuit of these: the right to vote, the right

to not be discriminated against on account of gender, that the whole feminist movement came into being. The Human Rights Act passed into law by the UK Parliament in 1998 and the apotheosis of the 'rights' movement, guarantees the 'right to life'. The Equality and Human Rights Commission website helpfully outlines what this means in practice:

> This means that nobody, including the Government, can try to end your life. It also means the Government should take appropriate measures to safeguard life by making laws to protect you and, in some circumstances, by taking steps to protect you if your life is at risk.

One day this 'right to life' might come to be understood, as logically it should, to apply as much to the child in the womb as it does to everyone else in their everyday lives. In the US, much of the current debate is precisely about the human rights of the foetus and what protection, if any, the US constitution confers on it. One day the US Supreme Court will have to decide the matter; Roe v. Wade, the 1973 Supreme Court ruling that established legal abortion in the US, reflected judicial opinion at that moment in time. Since then the debate has raged, opinions have changed and more conservative supreme justices have been appointed. Already the ground is shifting: an increasing number of US states are passing laws restricting abortion and the current US administration under President

Trump has made clear its intention to further the pro-life agenda. If the US does change its position, and if the Supreme Court decides that a foetus is deserving of the protection of the constitution, the UK might also then reopen the debate. If that happens it will be in the teeth of opposition from feminists who will be able to rely on the wholehearted support of the BBC. Abortion is another issue where the BBC's 'impartiality' turns out to be wholly theoretical.

Kimberlé Williams Crenshaw's theory of intersectionality remains, I suspect, unknown territory to most people, and yet it gives a label to a phenomenon which has been in plain sight for many years and long pre-dates her theorising: the tendency of transgressive campaigns to travel the political highway, as it were, in convoy. Intersectionality explains why it is that listening to or watching BBC output many people feel they are being led by the nose in a certain direction. It is why a clearly harmful and unbalanced idea like gender theory is implicitly embraced by the BBC, instead of being laughed out of court. Gender theory originated from the work of Sandra Bem, an American academic psychologist who set her mind to thinking about how it is that human beings develop a sense of gender. How do we come to know how to be male or female? An early supporter of the women's liberation movement (as feminism was colloquially known in the 1960s), there was little previous work on this subject. Bem, who as a child had witnessed violent fights between her parents, posited that many factors are in play in the formation of an individual's gender. She rejected the notion that gender is determined solely by biology, arguing that many other factors, especially parental and societal expectations are of crucial importance. Clearly gender is a legitimate and fascinating area of research for psychologists, but what is important to bear in mind is that Bem started with a very definite agenda; she believed that traditional male and female roles are harmfully restrictive for many individuals.

Her theory (and it remains just that – an intellectual conjecture) implanted in the public consciousness the insidious idea that parents are somehow wrong to raise their son or daughter in the traditional pattern of boy or girl. One might argue that this line of thinking has yielded some good things (both girls and boys have been encouraged to seek careers they find compatible, even if they are traditionally spheres dominated by the other gender), but it has also caused confusion, particularly in young men. It is not mere hyperbole to say that there is a crisis of masculinity in many Western societies. Bem's work was seminal, and it has seeped into mainstream thinking in a way which illustrates how social liberals have come to dominate the public debate while marginalising other viewpoints.

On the face of it campaigns in favour of abortion, or transgender rights, or against the deportation of terrorists on the grounds that their 'human rights' would thereby be infringed, do not have much in common. But Williams Crenshaw's idea explains exactly why they are all, in some way, part of a loosely bound caravan of political campaigns. In the minds of feminists like Williams Crenshaw there is a 'matrix of oppression' that conjures into being various victim groups, including men who want to become women, terrorists and, indeed, any other oppressed group of whom feminists approve. What binds these groups together is not any coherent campaign platform; it is, rather, a common enemy. And the common enemy is social conservatism which, in the Western context, means traditional Christian values.

The BBC was an early convert to second wave feminism and it has never wavered in its support; the third wave has been eagerly adopted too. But, whereas the early aims of the movement seemed to most people proper and relatively modest (fair treatment for female workers, equal educational opportunities etc.) and, indeed were consonant with Christian teachings about the worth and dignity of each individual, no brake has yet been applied to check the progressive momentum. Flushed with victory, the feminist cadres embraced ever more extreme campaigns based on a dogmatic interpretation of human rights. There are some crucial things to understand about this process, and the most important aspect is that it is the militants who arrogate to themselves the power to decide which campaigns will be accepted into the intersectional fold, and those that never will be.

Which is why gay rights are very much okay, but the rights, say, of conservative religious groups to hold to their own beliefs and act accordingly, will never be in the intersectional big tent. The way in which protection is offered to favoured groups – selected because they fit into the left's narrative of victimhood – is deeply unfair and long in evidence. A very clear example, from three decades ago, came during the miners' strike in the 1980s when the National Council for Civil Liberties (now known as Liberty) was put on the spot by those miners who stoutly maintained that they wanted to keep on working. An inquiry by the NCCL – which has always been a creature of the left – decided that while the police had infringed the civil rights of the strikers, the non-striking miners had rights too; the report included the following declaration which proved hugely controversial: 'freedom not to take part in a strike is as much a fundamental right as the right to strike'. This noble attempt to state a universal principle was too much for many NCCL members and at the subsequent AGM the inquiry team was found to have gone beyond its remit. Members of the inquiry, along with the general secretary, Larry Gostin, resigned. By standing up for the right to keep working, as well as the right to strike, the NCCL did what one might expect an organisation dedicated to upholding the rights of the individual to do. But that would be to misunderstand the radical nature of the group. It concerned itself selectively to defending, or establishing certain rights for approved victim groups. The NCCL always had a strong political agenda and campaigns for the rights of groups not seen as sympathetic to that agenda were never championed. The non-striking miners of 1984 did not fit the ideology and this episode – one among many – is why organisations like NCCL, now Liberty, are often treated with some circumspection by social conservatives: they are seen as left-wing campaign groups exclusively devoted to furthering a left-wing agenda.

The noble lie at the heart of all this is that life is made better for everyone – and could be better yet still – if only we would accept the inherent goodness and rightness of these myriad campaigns. But this is a plain falsehood. Many of the campaigns for the rights of various victim groups end up infringing the rights of others when success is achieved. In practice, this is often the case already, with the majority helplessly looking on as the protection of the law is given to groups who most people think are undeserving. People are left seething with indignation at the way the law is manipulated by someone like Abu Qatada, a jihadist preacher, who successfully delayed his deportation to Jordan for six years by skilful use of the Human Rights Act before the government finally prevailed in 2013. Ordinary citizens are at a loss to understand why people who are clearly up to no good can frustrate actions clearly aimed at protecting the public, all in the name of an individual's human rights. Over the long term this leads to a profound sense of alienation from the law, which ever more comes to be seen as the preserve of a social elite who care nothing for the views of 'ordinary people', but are dogmatic in their defence of theoretical rights which are never balanced by corresponding responsibilities. The common-sense view of a citizen's rights is that they have, in some way, to be earned: if you are a bad citizen then you should forfeit your rights, but that is not the way the law stands.

This is relevant to the debate about feminism because of the prerogatives it now claims – which have been willingly bestowed by the BBC and much of the rest of the media. Demands made in the name of feminism are granted a special status that shields them from challenge and scrutiny. Feminism is well-organised, vocal and fashionable; its opponents – such as they are – are none of these things, and so any counter-arguments that might be made go unheard. This has led us to an unhealthy place.

Militant feminism is corrosive of society because it elevates femaleness and denigrates maleness; it is not equality which is demanded, but superiority – as, for instance, in the matter of who gets to decide whether a baby should be aborted. 'Women and only women', say the feminists, because female decisions in this area are the only ones that count. Which, plainly, is discriminatory and wrong; men have a legitimate stake in these decisions and their views should also be taken into account.

A society which acts upon and enshrines feminist principles

will always be a divided society; militant feminism will guarantee that there is a permanent state of hostility between the sexes. If intersectionality theory is the guiding principle (which, in the BBC's case, it is) the (often irrational) demands of militant minorities will always trump the wishes of the majority. Social conservatives will always be the losers under this arrangement, as they have been for the past half-century. So far, the majority has remained quiescent. Often this is because of the bullying tactics of bigoted liberals who are masters of the techniques of media shaming; but this state of affairs will not last for ever. Social engineering pursued in the name of dangerous and half-baked theories will, at some point, create a backlash. This is already under way in some European countries, where it is labelled 'populism' by its liberal enemies. Up until now, the UK population has been sufficiently cowed to offer little resistance to deranged social theorists, but there is a mounting sense of unease about things like 'gender theory', and one day the worm will turn. Meanwhile, Auntie acts as the feminist ringmaster in all these debates, blind to her own partiality. A Sky News poll in early 2018 found that two thirds of Britons (67 per cent) feel feminism has either gone far enough or too far. Only 33 per cent felt feminism should go further.[10] Such a finding should give feminists pause for

---

10 See: https://news.sky.com/story/feminism-has-gone-far-enough-most-britons-say-11278752

thought, but probably won't. Certainly the BBC, convinced as always of her inability to do wrong, will plough on down the feminist track – all the while self-righteously proclaiming that Auntie doesn't have any favourites.

CHAPTER SEVEN

SUBMISSION: THE BBC
AND ISLAM

UNTIL 2001, THE COUNTRY at large tended to ignore
the growth of the Muslim community; unless you were
living in one of the areas to which south Asians had gravitated in
big numbers, it was something which was happening 'elsewhere'.
There were occasional grumbles one heard – rumours almost –
of trouble in some northern cities, but by and large, the Muslim
minority was invisible – just another component of Britain's
increasingly racially mixed society. That this was the case was, on
an optimistic reading, a reflection of traditional British tolerance
(there is a long history in these islands of immigrants arriving,
settling, being accepted and fitting in well); another way of
seeing it was that it reflected traditional British complacency.

The spring and summer of 2001 was an abrupt wake-up call to those who believed all was going swimmingly; the race riots which erupted in Oldham, Burnley and Bradford were the worst in Britain for many years, and they shattered the illusion that the official doctrine of multiculturalism was proving a resounding success. There were differences in the proximate cause of the riots in each place (the latter two probably had a copycat element about them), but the differences were superficial; underlying each one was a racial divide with Muslim Asians on one side and whites on the other.

Race riots in Britain are hardly unknown – in 1958, for instance, there was a riot in Notting Hill with whites on one side and West Indians on the other – and it is very probable that the 2001 riots, like those before them, might come to have been seen as a mere blip in a story of peaceful assimilation. Except that these riots were different. Firstly, they weren't markers of a racial divide determined by skin colour, but one determined by something less tangible and less tractable – a deep cultural difference underpinned by differing religious traditions; and secondly, they marked the beginning of a realisation that previous patterns of immigrant assimilation were unlikely to be repeated in the case of Britain's rapidly growing Muslim minority. Two months after the riot in Bradford came Al-Qaeda's attack on the Twin Towers in New York on 11 September 2001. That date now stands as the marker stone between two eras; pre-9/11 – an age of innocence when Islam

could be viewed as just another, largely benign, religious tradition (though a big and important one) – and post-9/11 when
the world woke up to some uncomfortable facts about the
growing perversion of Islam by Islamist extremists.

To the majority of people in Western countries, the idea that
some Muslims saw themselves at war with the West, and, what
is more, justified in their aggression, came as an unwelcome
surprise. It seemed to hark back to an earlier age of European
history when an aggressive expansionist Islam marched to the
very gates of Vienna and Christendom felt imperilled. Lulled
by the bromides of multiculturalism into a false sense of how
Western society was inevitably going to develop, this new and
unforeseen conflict set people scrambling for their reference
books to answer the question: 'Why?'

At the time, I was a reporter for *Today* on BBC Radio Four,
and, after it transpired that the 9/11 hijackers were nearly all
Saudis, I started looking at Wahhabism – the austere strain
of Islam which emerged out of the sands of the Arabian
Peninsula in the eighteenth century. Thanks to an alliance
between Muhammad ibn Abd al-Wahhab, the founder of
the movement, and Muhammad bin Saud, an ancestor of the
current King of Saudi Arabia, Wahhabism grew to become
the official, state-sponsored version of the faith throughout
the kingdom. My modest package on *Today* attempted to fill
in the background for an audience scrambling to understand
more about Islam. The authorities in Saudi Arabia deny there is

any such thing as Wahhabism: the austere version of Islam they practice, they claim, is the Islam of the Salaf – the generation of the Prophet and his followers. It is a somewhat academic point; all Wahhabis – that is those who follow the teachings and practice of al-Wahhab – are Salafis, but not all Salafis are Wahhabis. Salafism, a movement that began in Egypt and came into Saudi Arabia during the reign of King Faisal, is claimed to be quiet and non-political. There is now intense competition between groups and individual scholars over the 'true' Salafism. The easy explanation for differences within the Salafi movement is that some aim to change society through da'wah (preaching/evangelising), whereas others want to change it through violence.

My quick journalistic investigation suggested that Wahhabism was a natural seedbed for fanaticism, and thus not a very promising partner in the multicultural future our government had planned for us. As it turns out, I didn't know the half of it: Wahhabism, and its blood-brother Salafism, are the very antithesis of multiculturalism, and eventually that fashionable theory crumbled, a victim of the collision between Islam and Western values. To take but one of the significant differences; Islam does not allow for apostasy – that is the renunciation of one's personal faith or conversion to another religion. Whereas in the West we have long acknowledged that the individual is absolutely free to decide for themselves whether to follow a religion or not, in Islam no such free choice is allowed. Apostasy is viewed as both a sin and a religious crime. People are still executed in Islamic countries for the 'crime' of apostasy. As recently as 2015 a man was executed in Saudi Arabia for apostasy, and nothing more clearly underlines the gulf of understanding between Islam and the West. The uncompromising and intransigent nature of Islam left the BBC – the cheerleader-in-chief for multiculturalism – in an awkward spot. Untroubled, as usual, by self-doubt, the Corporation had for years blithely promoted a blueprint for the country where immigrant cultures maintained their separate identities; the 'nation' was to become merely a shared geographical space with the traditional culture now merely first among equals. What could possibly go wrong?

Multiculturalism as a term originated in Canada in the 1950s as a snappier alternative to 'cultural pluralism', which was what Canadian politicians had started to talk about as a policy that could bridge the historic cultural divide in the country between the (majority) English-speakers and the (minority) Francophone population who mainly lived in Quebec province. And in those terms it seemed both eminently sensible and fair: as an advanced democracy, Canada was obliged to find some way of accommodating its French-speakers who had just as much right as the Anglos to inhabit the country. Multiculturalism was the theory that buttressed that necessary accommodation. The social theorists then extended the idea to embrace the tribal cultures of the aboriginal peoples who lived on the north American landmass before European colonisation; today these are referred to as the 'First Nations' in common Canadian discourse. What was unforeseen was the way in which this doctrine, when exported to other parts of the world, would become a cultural Trojan horse, harnessed by leftists to undermine assumptions about national identity and the rights of the majority.

The Canadian notion of multiculturalism was grounded in a social reality. Francophone Canadians, though a minority, had an undeniable right to cultural equality with their Anglophone neighbours; both populations were the descendants of colonisers who had inhabited the land for roughly the same length of time, and both cultures were equally advanced and sophisticated. Though some Francophone separatists wanted independence for their part of Canada, there was nothing fundamentally incompatible about the two cultural streams which both had roots in European culture.[1] Official parity of esteem between the two communities, though in some ways irksome to the majority (officially mandated bilingualism is disliked by many) was justified on both practical and moral grounds. But the cultural equivalence implicit in the Canadian situation was rooted in a particular set of circumstances where two cultural traditions of equal worth sat alongside each other.

---

1   Referendums on sovereignty for Quebec, demanded by the Parti Québécois were held in 1980 and 1995. Both were defeated although the second one only very narrowly.

The activists who seized on multiculturalism as a mechanism to disrupt national cultures in other countries had no such justification. The idea that all cultures are of equal worth – which is how multiculturalism came to be interpreted in Britain – is pernicious and wrong. The example of female genital mutilation shows why.

FGM is a procedure whereby pre-pubertal girls are 'cut' – that is they have their clitoris and sometime parts of the labia removed. It's a practice, recorded in antiquity, but which still persists, particularly in sub-Saharan Africa. It is a painful and unnecessary procedure done in the name of chastity, but which can lead to all sorts of unpleasant medical consequences. It was made unlawful in Britain in 1985 (British Christian missionaries led a campaign against it in Africa as far back as the 1930s), but has proved stubbornly difficult to stamp out. FGM is an example of a practice, deemed normal and indeed desirable in some cultures, but which our Western culture views as barbaric and primitive. A country like Britain does not need to apologise for outlawing FGM – most British people would expect no less; FGM is simply wrong and no amount of special pleading about cultural preferences can obscure the fact. Furthermore, any objective comparison between a culture that allows FGM and one that forbids it would conclude that the latter is superior to the former. That is because by prohibiting FGM the law is being used to protect the innocent victims. There is no need to be mealy-mouthed about this: in some important regards Western culture really is superior.

The heyday of multiculturalism in Britain came in the late 1990s and extended into the new century. Perhaps the high-water mark came in October 2000 with the publication by the Runnymede Trust[2] of a report entitled *The Future of Multi-ethnic Britain*. The future this research, commissioned by then chairman of the trust Trevor Phillips, envisioned was that Britain would become a 'community of communities' where each separate 'community' would show 'respect' for every other 'community' by not giving offence. This was a period when multiculturalism had the support of Prime Minister Tony Blair and the entire government apparatus, and immense damage resulted. Not only was the culture of the majority diminished in status because, we were told, we had no right to expect it to be accorded any special value, but real crimes and abuses flourished, shielded as they were by a fierce political correctness.

What it permitted to take root, and to escape proper scrutiny from the police, the courts, social workers and even the medical profession, were a range of illegal and immoral practices that should never have been tolerated. So it was, for instance, that social workers and the police in Rotherham failed properly to investigate the systematic rape and sexual abuse of young, mainly white girls by a gang of Muslim men. It was not, of

---

2   The Runnymede Trust is a race equality think tank established in 1968.

course, that anyone, in a police station or social work office sat down and decided that it was okay for Muslim men to coerce young white girls into sex on some spurious cultural grounds; what happened was that the entirety of official Britain was cowed by a bullying cultural elite whose weapon of choice was to label any dissenter 'racist' – a term which has proved career-ending for scores of officials and politicians. The BBC, to its shame, was always eager to amplify allegations of that type and became, in effect, the enforcer-in-chief of this kind of mind control.

One of the striking things about the doctrine of multi-culturalism is that it arose and became dominant without ever having the true consent of the public; it was never properly explained and it was foisted on the country by political parties who gave little thought to its implications. It was a theory which first gained a foothold with social theorists in universities, spread rapidly among left-wing political activists and became the received wisdom among the media class. Implicit in multi-culturalism is the idea that Western culture is uniquely and inherently racist and unfair; multiculturalism, it should be understood, is deeply anti-Western. In this view of the world, the West's original sin was colonialism; in the view of many on the left, colonialism equates to the sin against the Holy Ghost – that which can never be forgiven. This way of thinking requires the former colonisers – Britain foremost among them – to commit to endless reparations to the countries which were colonised. Britain's large (and by international comparison relatively generous) aid budget is handed over partly because it is a way of assuaging our colonial guilt. And there is another way the reparations are made, through cultural abasement; we denigrate our own culture while extending uncritical admiration and support to foreign cultures which are often deeply repressive and corrupt. There is a profound irony in this because it is only in Western cultures – which cherish and guarantee free thinking and free speech – that an idea like multiculturalism can be discussed and adopted: the individual who tries to do the same thing in an authoritarian society – China, say, or any number of other countries, is likely to fall foul of the authorities and suffer the consequences.

The appeal of multiculturalism to the left – when rigorously applied – was that it subverted traditional culture and so became a useful weapon in the battle against 'the forces of conservatism' (in Tony Blair's vivid, and somewhat sinister, phrase[3]).

---

3   From Blair's speech to the Labour conference in 1999. This is the key passage: 'A New Britain where the extraordinary talent of the British people is liberated from the forces of conservatism that so long have held them back, to create a model twenty-first century nation, based not on privilege, class or background, but on the equal worth of all. And New Labour, confident at having modernised itself, now the new progressive force in British politics which can modernise the nation, sweep away those forces of conservatism to set the people free. One hundred years in existence, twenty-two in power, we have never, ever won a full second term. That is our unfinished business. Let us now finish it and with it finish the Tory Party's chances of doing as much damage in the next century as they've done in this one. Today's Tory Party – the party of fox hunting, Pinochet and hereditary peers: the uneatable, the unspeakable and the unelectable.'

And, because it came cloaked in the language of equality, it was difficult to argue against. How do you (politely) frame an argument which, in effect, says to immigrant minorities, 'the culture of this land is better than that of your homeland – that's probably why you came here – and if you come here to live with us you must get with the programme'. If you do try making an argument in those terms, it is all too easy for your political opponents to smear you as a smug racist and an insensitive cultural triumphalist; during the years of the Blair supremacy it became almost impossible publicly to stand against the multicultural tide. That tide only turned, and only then rhetorically, when the malign consequences of multiculturalism became too obvious to ignore, and some of its promoters bravely began to acknowledge that it was causing dangerous problems in the real world.

By 2004 there were straws in the wind; an important one appeared in the bien-pensant magazine of choice *Prospect*, in an article penned by that magazine's founder David Goodhart. Goodhart, hitherto a stalwart of progressive values, sounded a warning note in an article headlined 'Too Diverse?', which questioned whether a high-spending welfare state was sustainable above a certain level of racial and cultural diversity. Here is a key passage from the article:

> Immigrants from the same place are bound to want to congregate together but policy should try to prevent

that consolidating into segregation across all the main areas of life: residence, school, workplace, church. In any case, the laissez-faire approach of the post-war period in which ethnic minority citizens were not encouraged to join the common culture (although many did) should be buried. Citizenship ceremonies, language lessons and the mentoring of new citizens should help to create a British version of the old US melting pot. This third way on identity can be distinguished from the coercive assimilations of the nationalist right, which rejects any element of foreign culture, and from multiculturalism, which rejects a common culture.[4]

Goodhart's reasoning was informed by research like that of Harvard professor of political science Robert D. Putnam. He is the author of the hugely influential book *Bowling Alone* (2000), which detailed declining levels of social capital and community fragmentation in the US. In 2001, Putnam published data from a decade-long research project into how increasing levels of diversity affected the levels of social trust; broadly speaking, what he found was that the greater the racial and cultural diversity of a population, the lower the levels of trust in that community. Professor Putnam concluded that people in diverse communities 'don't trust the local mayor,

4 David Goodhart, 'Too diverse?', *Prospect* magazine, February 2004.

they don't trust the local paper, they don't trust other people and they don't trust institutions'. He concludes: 'The effect of diversity is worse than had been imagined. And it's not just that we don't trust people who are not like us. In diverse communities, we don't trust people who do look like us.' For David Goodhart the realisation that increased diversity, the inescapable consequence of mass immigration, could erode social solidarity and hence imperil a welfare state paid for out of taxes, was reason enough to sound a warning note.

The reception his article received on the left was hysterically negative. There was strident criticism from Trevor Phillips, who said that Goodhart's comments might have come from a British National Party blogger (and there could be no more hurtful an insult from a man ensconced at the very pinnacle of the liberal-left journalistic elite). But then, amazingly, Mr Phillips underwent a Damascene conversion of his own: just a few months later in a dramatic move he denounced his own report – 'The Future of Multi-ethnic Britain' – saying he now realised it encouraged 'separatism'. Interviewed many years later Mr Phillips had this to say about it:

> Well I think it would be fair to say that I made a big mis-
> take. It was a clear statement that some groups can play
> by their own rules. That to me runs counter to my own
> political beliefs. Why I am still a supporter of the Labour
> Party is because I believe fundamentally in solidarity and

reciprocity, and I think most on the left have forgotten both of those things.[5]

That two prominent figures in the liberal elite had and renounced their belief in multiculturalism – hitherto a sacred cow – was a sure sign that the wheels were coming off the bandwagon, though much damage had already been done. The instinct to protect the rights of immigrants is wholesome and good; any individual moving to a new country is likely to face many difficulties of acculturation. Such people deserve the same respect as anyone else; it is right that they should be shielded, by law, from discrimination, and that they should be offered a helping hand by the authorities. But what is clearly wrong is that the host community should be expected to tolerate, indeed encourage, the growth of communities who live by a different set of rules from the majority; that is no recipe for cultural harmony. The multicultural ideal of a patchwork quilt of different ethnic groups living side by side, each respecting the others' differences, is a utopian fantasy that can all too easily degenerate into a system of ethnic Bantustans with no trust – and sometimes outright hostility – between them. What is more, such a system is almost certain to arouse the suspicions of the majority who see the growth in their midst of unfamiliar cultures which are likely to appear both impenetrable and potentially hostile.

---

5 Interview with Trevor Phillips, *The Guardian*, 19 February 2017.

The growth of multiculturalism in the 1990s went hand in hand with a rigid political correctness, indeed, the two are inseparable. The notion of something being 'politically correct' arose out of Marxist discourse; in those great Marxist test-beds, the Soviet Union and China, the cadres – that is the activists – were subject to regular interrogations by political commissars to make sure that their ideas were not straying from the line approved by the Party leadership. Any deviation from this 'correct' line could have fearsome consequences; 're-education' at best, execution at worst. Some Western apologists for political correctness say that in our societies it is not sinister, it is only a matter, they claim, of being polite and of shaming people into not using words that minority groups find offensive. If that was all that PC amounted to, it could indeed be seen as benevolent, but in the hands of zealots it became a potent weapon to close down necessary debates.

If you can't find the language to talk about a problem, for fear of being pounced upon and belittled by some PC enforcer, it will be left to fester. Which is precisely what seems to have happened in the case of the Muslim rape gangs who have now been discovered operating in at least sixteen British towns and cities.[6]

---

6 Gangs of Muslim men who have groomed and abused young girls have been prosecuted in Rochdale, Rotherham, Oxford, Telford, Leeds, Birmingham, Norwich, Burnley, High Wycombe, Leicester, Dewsbury, Middlesbrough, Peterborough, Bristol, Halifax and Newcastle. There are other prosecutions pending.

So nervous were individual police officers, social workers and politicians of offending against the axioms of politically correct multiculturalism that for far too long they remained silent. Political correctness is a pharisaical creed, shot through with self-righteous hypocrisy; it is a way of intimidating and demonising political opponents for verbal infelicities, while allowing terrible wrongs to go unaddressed. It is the hand-maiden of multiculturalism, and no organisation has been more assiduous in promoting its tenets and policing and punishing those who transgress than the BBC.

As mentioned in a previous chapter, the BBC has closed down debate on many issues that are important to social conservatives; on things like abortion, divorce and gay rights, the BBC does not willingly allow dissident voices to be heard although, in truth, these are issues where people in a free society should be allowed to exercise freedom of speech – and conscience. The fact that the law says that abortion, or homosexuality, is okay does not make them morally good choices in the eyes of those who oppose the practice of both – rather, in their eyes, it underlines just how immoral the law can be. The favoured tactic of the modern-day pharisees is to disparage their opponents rather than engaging with their argument. So anyone who opposes abortion is a 'bigot', a term which ends debate. A special lexicon has been developed comprising a short list of words which are used to vilify social conservatives; it includes racist, homophobe, misogynist and

Islamophobe. By deploying these terms it is possible to undermine the credentials of anyone making a counterargument and then to justify denying them opportunities to explain their position.

And it is this tactic which has been used to throw the BBC's protective mantle over Islam; if you are a critic of that faith you become an 'Islamophobe', which squeezes out the possibility that fear of Islam might be a rational reaction to the events of the past couple of decades (to say nothing of the historical record).

This is not to argue that there are no people who merit these descriptions. There are people who do actually hate people of other races; there are some who have a violent hatred of homosexuality, there are men who despise women and, yes, there are some people who hate Muslims. But having misgivings about mass immigration does not make you racist, having moral qualms about homosexuality does not make you homophobic; refusing to accept radical feminist ideology does not make you misogynist and fearing aspects of Islam does not make you Islamophobic.

To understand why the BBC has ruthlessly closed down any proper understanding of Islam, it is necessary to recall Kimberlé Williams Crenshaw's doctrine of intersectionality and to understand how it applies to Islam. Here is the Oxford Living Dictionary definition of the creed that now informs the BBC's whole philosophy. Intersectionality is:

The interconnected nature of social categorizations such as race, class, and gender as they apply to a given individual or group, regarded as creating overlapping and interdependent systems of discrimination or disadvantage.

Immediately one can see how Britain's Muslim community is a perfect fit for inclusion in the intersectional victim narrative. It is a fact that some of Britain's roughly three million Muslims (around 5 per cent of the population) are disadvantaged; one possible common-sense explanation for that, could be that originally they were mainly poor people who came from underdeveloped parts of the world, lacking good education and settling in parts of the UK where they took low-status jobs in declining industries. Some of the descendants of those original immigrants have grasped the opportunities British society offers to better their lot, but some have not, and so there are some British Muslims who remain poor. At this point, proponents of politically correct multiculturalism step in to argue that the fault for this lies with the prejudice of their British hosts and their unfair discrimination against Muslims. Using this argument, the 'Muslim Community' can be enlisted, wholesale, into the 'victim' category where, safely ensconced, the BBC shields it from criticism. Victim status gives you an imperviable shelter from media scrutiny or attack.

However, the real national debate about Islam (that is, the debate which ordinary citizens need to engage in – not the 'official' debate, as defined by the BBC and the rest of the mainstream media) is not about the wrongs suffered by Britain's Muslim minority, it is about the nature of Islam itself and how – if at all – it can be integrated into British society. When Muslim fanatics blew up a bus and a tube train in 2005, when they decapitated Fusilier Lee Rigby in 2013, when they planted a bomb to slaughter children attending a concert in Manchester in 2017, the question uppermost in people's minds was not how poverty and disadvantage pertained to these atrocities; rather it was how Islam itself could inspire people to do such dreadful acts. And, despite BBC presenters endlessly repeating the question, 'How have these good Muslims become radicalised?', we are no nearer hearing a truthful answer.

The reason we are no nearer an understanding is because the fearful truth is one that very few people – and none, it seems in the BBC – wish to face up to. The incontestable fact is that Islam's holy book, the Koran, has passages in it which can be, and regularly are, used to justify violence against unbelievers – the 'kafir' in the Koran's own usage. There is a huge volume of scholarship and literature on this subject and many of the authorities disagree with each other about the precise translations of the Koranic verses and what they actually mean; this book is not the place to enter that debate in detail. It will suffice here to quote a couple of the best-known Koranic verses which do seem, on a plain reading, to articulate a very negative view of Christians and Jews.

Oh you who believe! Do not take the Jews and the Christians for friends. They are the friends of each other and
whoever amongst you takes them for a friend, then, surely
he is one of them; surely Allah does not guide the unjust
people. [Sura 5, verse 51]

And again:

Whoever is the enemy of Allah and his angels and his
apostles and Jibreel and Meekaeel, so surely Allah is the
enemy of the unbelievers. [Sura 2, verse 98]

There are many other Koranic verses, scores in fact, that make
reference to Jews and Christians – and few of them seem to put
forward a positive view. Some Islamic scholars maintain that,
actually, Islam has always taken a benign view of the 'people
of the book', as Jews and Christians are sometimes known to
Muslims. But it is too easy to get bogged down in scholarly
interpretations; a more straightforward way of understanding
what is going on is to look at the record of recent years and what
terrorists, acting in the name of Islam, have said and done.
The cruelty and bloodthirstiness of the Islamic State towards
'unbelievers' is surely evidence enough of the Koran's malign
influence on those who fight in Islam's name.

The BBC has always shied away from acknowledging this
obvious fact: its mealy-mouthed formulation, 'the so-called

Islamic State' is clear evidence that the Corporation is in a state of denial about the phenomenon we are facing. The Muslim warriors fighting their jihad in Syria and Iraq had no illusions about what they were fighting for and why; they did not attempt to dissimulate about their intentions or their view of themselves. When they said that theirs was the Islamic State, based on revealed Islamic truth, and fighting for a modern incarnation of an Islamic caliphate, there seems little reason not to take them at their word. But the BBC knows better; its view seems to be that the Islamic State cannot be truly Islamic because the BBC's own understanding of Islam showed it to be a 'religion of peace'. Which is, when you consider the matter, peculiarly arrogant – as if the BBC itself has a clearer insight into the nature of Islam than the people who go out to kill and die for it. When the Soviet Union was a going concern, the BBC did not dub it the 'so-called Communist state' to spare the feelings of Marxists. And yet, it constantly panders to Muslim sentiment by refusing to countenance the possibility (now, given the evidence, the overwhelming likelihood) that Islam inspires some of its fanatical adherents to commit evil acts. The BBC accepted the USSR at face value as the Communist state it claimed to be, warts and all. Not so the case with the Islamic State. Instead, at every opportunity, the BBC parroted the claim that Islam is a 'religion of peace' – a bromide that the people of the Western world were surely tiring of hearing as the body count rose ever higher.

In line with the dictates of the secularist dogma that now informs every aspect of the BBC's world view, the Corporation does not go out of its way to distinguish between the world's religions; it has lost the faculty of proper discrimination, informed by a shared national morality, so that now it considers all religions to be of equal worth. Or, one might more accurately say, that it views all religions as equally worthless – mere superstitions with little to choose between them. This may be down to simple ignorance on behalf of a generation of BBC people who do not know, nor care, about what distinguishes Christianity, say, from Islam. However, only the most intransigent and dogmatic secularists could possibly maintain that the differences between the two are not profound and fundamental. The differences are clearly there in the foundational texts of the two belief systems and they are clearly manifested in the historical record. So it is that Jesus Christ never, at any point, is shown in scripture to be anything other than a man of peace. At every point where violence might have been an option – when, for instance, he is taken prisoner in the Garden at Gethsemane on the night before his crucifixion – Jesus forbids it:

> Then Simon Peter having a sword drew it, and smote the high priest's servant, and cut off his right ear. The servant's name was Malchus. Then said Jesus unto Peter, Put up thy sword into the sheath: the cup which my Father hath given me, shall I not drink it? [John 18: 10–11]

According to Luke's gospel Jesus healed Malchus after the blow. This is but one incident – there are numerous others where Jesus calls on his followers to accept persecution in his name, but not themselves to persecute – 'turn the other cheek' etc. What is more, he makes it plain on many occasions that his message is for all mankind; he never stokes up antagonism between ethnic groups, but always seeks to heal and unite them. This truly denotes Christianity as a 'religion of peace' – no true Christian can find in the New Testament justification for violence or aggression. And, in one of the strangest and most important turning points in all of world history, this philosophy of humility and loving kindness came, via the Roman Empire, to dominate the West. It did so not by the sword but by converting men's hearts to the Christian truth.

This is not to gloss the historical record of Christianity. There have been terrible deeds done in its name, but the fact that some Christians have behaved badly in past centuries does not invalidate the central Christian message of peace. Yes 'Christian' armies have rampaged and slaughtered in the name of Christian rulers, but it is impossible to justify killing by reference to Christian scripture. In that important sense the Gospel story differs from the Koran.

Christianity became the religion of Europe not because of conquest, fire and sword but through the power of the compelling truths that it enunciates. Many of its first adherents, the Apostles of the gospel stories, ended up martyrs for their faith, killed for their beliefs. Their teachings, about the universal and inalienable dignity of each individual, about self-sacrifice and the love of others, about non-violence and acceptance of persecution as a way of bearing witness to the truth, proved to be strangely seductive in a Roman world which was martial and cruel.

Rome was a slave empire where the lives of the low-born counted for very little; Christianity was revolutionary because it taught that the Emperor and the slave are held to exactly the same moral standard. God, it taught, expected everyone to behave according to the precepts laid down by Jesus and to be judged accordingly; each person will eventually stand before their Creator and the record of their life will be examined and judged. This idea, that all our actions are known and that there will be a reckoning, proved the most potent of all, guiding countless millions of people down through the ages to do what is right, according to their conscience, informed by Christian teaching. Given that the teaching instructed individuals to be selfless and just towards all – even enemies – the amount of evildoing which has thus been prevented, because of Christian conscience, is incalculable. It should still be a matter of wonder that a small Jewish sect, inspired by a man who ended his days nailed to a cross for having preached a doctrine rooted in love for his fellow man, emerged from persecution and hiding to become the guiding philosophy of the West for the next two thousand years. And did so, not by force of arms, but by conversion in the privacy of human hearts.

The contrast with Islam is stark, and reveals much about that faith's troubled relationship with the modern world. The beginnings of Islam are poorly documented; there are very few, if any, reliable contemporaneous accounts. But from the fragmentary sources that do exist, the scholarly consensus is that in the seventh century AD a charismatic leader, who we know as Muhammad, came to the fore in the land of Arabia and united the tribes around him. He was a seer and a prophet and he claimed to have direct revelations from God which mandated new ways of living to his followers. Muhammad built this new faith on borrowings from both Jewish and Christian teaching, which, like Islam, teaches that there is only one God. However, although that one, central belief is common to all three religions, there are many points of disagreement. For instance, Christians believe that Jesus was, literally, the son of God – the 'word made flesh'; a man, but also God. Islam, while it acknowledges Jesus (Isa as he is known in the Koran) as a good man and a prophet, denies his divinity. This is not the place to attempt a disquisition on the doctrinal differences between Islam and Christianity – I am certainly not qualified for the task – but the spread of Islam after the death of Muhammad in 632 AD can quite easily be outlined.

Between 622 AD and 750 AD Islam spread from its original locality (around Mecca on the western side of the Arabian Peninsula) to dominate an area estimated at five million square miles. This encompassed the whole of the Arabia, and, to the east, the Levant and Persia right to the borders of present-day India; to the west Islam swept through north Africa to the Atlantic coast and then up through the Iberian Peninsula. It was, by any reckoning, a dramatically successful expansion achieved at the point of a sword.

The early successes of Islam were astonishing feats of arms and naturally threatening to the Christian kingdoms of the north and they set in train a long period of struggle between the two sides. Christendom attempted to recover lost territories through a series of crusades – reactive episodes which mostly ended in failure; Islam pressed forward always seeking to expand its territories and became the great 'other' for Christian Europe.

This epic confrontation, beginning as it did in Islam's earliest days, can and should be seen as the factor which more than any other shaped the western world down even to the present day. Looking now at current events in Europe and the Middle East who can deny that the skeleton outline of all the many bloody and calamitous conflicts of our own day were set centuries ago? The border between Islam and the rest are marked throughout the world, not just in Europe, by bloodshed. But this is a truth that many contemporary authorities, and certainly the BBC, do not wish to explore.

It is notable how rarely the BBC explains contemporary wars by reference to their historic roots involving Muslim/ Christian conflict; for instance, in 1999 when Tony Blair's government sent RAF bombers to punish Serbia and to deliver Kosovo to the (Muslim) Albanians, there was little attempt to understand the Serbian position; the BBC uncritically swallowed the government's line and set about demonising the Serbs. And yet Serbia has historically been one of the fault lines between Christianity and Islam, and the Serbs suffered centuries of subjugation by the Ottoman Turks. In a museum in Belgrade I once saw an exhibition of Ottoman atrocities from the nineteenth century; in one picture a highway was lined with crucified Serbian nationalists. Such cruelties do not rapidly fade from the national consciousness.

This squeamishness about exploring the historic origins of the contest between Christianity and Islam is a barrier to understanding the modern world. On the BBC's part it arises from its determination that the world should not be seen through the lens of an ancient antagonism even when that is the surest way of unlocking important truths about our current conflicts. What the BBC is particularly at pains to obscure is the profound differences there are between Islam and Christianity; partly that is because if those differences are explicitly laid out Islam suffers through the comparison. And yet this difference can, quite easily, be traced back to the gulf in character between the two individuals – Jesus and Muhammad – who are at the heart of the two religions. Jesus was, indisputably, a man of peace who ordered his followers to emulate his example and abjure violence; that many

Christians, and sometimes in spectacular ways, have failed to do so does not in any way invalidate Christ's simple message. Anyone who sincerely models themselves on Christ will be a peaceable individual devoted to the welfare of his fellow man. What sort of model, by comparison, does Muhammad offer?

William Muir was a nineteenth-century British scholar who devoted a large part of his life to first understanding and then writing about Islam and the life of Muhammad. His four-volume *Life of Mahomet* (1861) was the first comprehensive and learned account published in English and – even today – many modern scholars acknowledge it as a useful source. Here is one passage, Muir's judgement after a lifetime of study, that sheds light on the man who was Muhammad:

> Magnanimity or moderation are nowhere discernible as features in the conduct of Mahomet towards such of his enemies as failed to tender a timely allegiance. Over the bodies of the Coreish who fell at Badr, he exulted with savage satisfaction; and several prisoners,—accused of no crime but that of scepticism and political opposition,— were deliberately executed at his command. The Prince of Kheibar, after being subjected to inhuman torture for the purpose of discovering the treasures of his tribe, was, with his cousin, put to death on the pretext of having treacherously concealed them: and his wife was led away captive to the tent of the conqueror ... And what is perhaps worst

of all, the dastardly assassination of political and religious opponents, countenanced and frequently directed as they were in all their cruel and perfidious details by Mahomet himself, leaves a dark and indelible blot upon his character.[7]

Muhammad's relationship with women was not a sudden departure from pre-Islamic Bedouin culture in which polygamy was a standard feature. But the example the Prophet gave in his dealings with women left a deep imprint on the faith he originated; the Koran contains a number of passages where it is clear that women should be subordinate to men:

> Men have authority over women because God has made the one superior to the other, and because they spend their wealth to maintain them. Good women are obedient. They guard their unseen parts because God has guarded them. As for those from whom you fear disobedience, admonish them, forsake them in beds apart, and beat them.
> [Sura 4:34]

This is plainly very different from the Christian tradition as regards men and how they should treat women; as a useful comparison, here is what Jesus said about marriage and divorce:

---

7   William Muir, *Life of Mahomet*, Volume IV (1861), pp. 307–309.

The Pharisees also came to Him, testing Him, and saying to Him, 'Is it lawful for a man to divorce his wife for just any reason?' And He answered and said to them, 'Have you not read that He who made them at the beginning "made them male and female,"' and said, 'For this reason a man shall leave his father and mother and be joined to his wife, and the two shall become one flesh'? So then, they are no longer two but one flesh. Therefore what God has joined together, let not man separate. [Matthew 19:3–6, new King James Version]

In Victorian times, when scholars like William Muir were first getting to grips with Muslim history and theology there was a clear understanding of the disadvantages of Muslim teaching as compared with Christianity. Today our media generally, and the BBC in particular, have lost, it seems, the confidence to discriminate between the two. That is what happens if you sign up to the multicultural doctrine where every culture (and the word, of course, embraces religious tradition) is on an equal footing. Muir, by contrast, was very clear about what he identified as Islam's 'three radical evils':

First: Polygamy, Divorce, and Slavery strike at the root of public morals, poison domestic life, and disorganise society; while the Veil removes the female sex from its just position and influence in the world. Second: freedom of thought and private judgment are crushed and annihilated. Toleration is unknown, and the possibility of free and liberal institutions foreclosed. Third: a barrier has been interposed against the reception of Christianity.[8]

And yet, in what must surely rank as one of the most unnatural of all ideological couplings, British feminists have been among the first to leap to the defence of Islam, brandishing allegations of 'Islamophobia' against anyone who criticises Muslim practice. A piece from *The Guardian* in 2013 by feminist writer Laurie Penny is typical of the genre. Headlined 'This isn't "feminism". It's Islamophobia' the sub-heading reads, 'I am infuriated by white men stirring up anti-Muslim prejudice to derail debate on western sexism'. Here's the opening paragraph:

> As a person who writes about women's issues, I am constantly being told that Islam is the greatest threat to gender equality in this or any other country – mostly by white men, who always know best. This has been an extraordinary year for feminism, but from the Rochdale grooming case to interminable debates over whether traditional Islamic dress is 'empowering' or otherwise, the rhetoric and language of feminism has been co-opted by

---

8   William Muir, ibid.

Islamophobes, who could not care less about women of any creed or colour.[9]

Given that in some Muslim communities traditional Muslim practice involves female genital mutilation, the attitude of feminists like Ms Penny might seem perverse; surely, one might think, modern feminists should be the first to condemn a religion which condones such barbarity?

This puzzling perversity of the feminist movement only becomes intelligible when one grasps the full implications of 'intersectionality'. The true-believing intersectionalist feminist will have already incorporated multiculturalism into her core beliefs which means that she is obliged to come to the defence of any group which can plausibly be portrayed as a vulnerable minority. Muslim women, obliged by custom to don the hijab or, in more rigorous communities, the burqa, are thus taken under the wing of Britain's feminist movement. The amount of doublethink necessary here is astonishing; Western feminists often sound off about the way in which they are 'objectified' by Western culture, which is portrayed as coercive and oppressive, and yet at the same time they are heard to argue that Muslim women should be allowed to dress in robes of 'modesty' because that is their choice. An organisation called the European Network

---

9   Laurie Penny, 'This isn't "feminism". It's Islamophobia', *The Guardian*, 22 December 2013.

Against Racism has produced a leaflet entitled 'Debunking Myths on Women's Rights, Muslim Women, Feminism and Islamophobia in Europe', which gives a stout feminist defence of Islamic dress codes. Announcing as its intention 'to better address intersectional discrimination against Muslim women', part of the section on Islamic dress codes reads as follows:

> One can't systematically dismiss free choice just because one assumes that this choice is an internalisation of patriarchy. We can question how patriarchy made it possible for the headscarf to become a symbol of modesty for women, but we could equally question a lot of decisions made by women. The issue of choice is also important for feminists as each woman's agency and right to choose, but we also must see that choice happens within an overall system of patriarchy which oppresses women.[10]

Untangling what exactly this means is quite difficult – do women who have 'internalised the patriarchy' actually have free choice? But even leaving this aside, it seems odd for Western feminists to stand up for a rigid dress code imposed by religious authorities, something which, clearly they would never accept for themselves.

---

10 'Debunking Myths on Women's Rights, Muslim Women, Feminism and Islamophobia in Europe', European Network Against Racism, 7 July 2017.

What real choice there might be in a culture where holy writ orders women to cover up is not up for discussion. The Koran says: 'O Prophet, tell your wives and your daughters and the women of the believers to bring down over themselves of their outer garments. That is more suitable that they will be known and not be abused. And ever is Allah Forgiving and Merciful.' (33:59). The implication is that if women do not cover themselves adequately with their outer garments, they may be abused, and that such abuse would be justified.

Taking Islam's part in these arguments is, of course, really a way of further undermining 'the enemy', which was originally, and remains, Christianity; one of the many baseless charges laid against Christianity by feminism is that it is sternly patriarchal and subjugates women. Feminism is deeply opposed to the Christian Church and has been one of its most potent enemies. In concert with other transgressive movements it has managed to replace a morality based on the dignity and human equality of each person, male or female, with a new morality which shape-shifts according to fashion. No Christian man can, in good conscience, treat his wife as an inferior, still less beat her; if he does he would be sinning against God. Also, and importantly, it is impossible to find any justification for wife-beating in the New Testament – because no such textual justification exists.

It is true that Christianity elevates the role of 'father' and to that extent is 'patriarchal'; but a Christian patriarch acts with loving kindness at all times – tyrannical patriarchy is profoundly anti-Christian. Then again, Christian strictures against divorce are viewed negatively by feminists who argue that women must be freed from any constraints in this area. But easy divorce is a great danger to women, as Christianity has always recognised; in the UK it has resulted in millions of them being abandoned by men, the fathers of their children, and left to fend for themselves. Is that feminist progress?

Islam has set down deep roots in Britain; there are now around three million Muslims living in the country, and their numbers are growing fast thanks to high birth rates and continuing immigration. The picture is the same across the rest of Europe; everywhere the number of Muslims in our midst is rising quickly. For the most part these fellow citizens are law-abiding and peaceable, but that should not blind us to the challenges that the current situation brings with it. In his ground-breaking book *The Strange Death of Europe: Immigration, Identity, Islam*,[11] Douglas Murray charts, in forensic detail, what has happened in Europe in recent decades. His book depicts Europe sleepwalking into a period of change of the most profound kind; as Murray sees it, Europe is in the process of jettisoning the shared certainties of a culture deeply informed by Christianity, which arose from the continent's

---

11 Douglas Murray, *The Strange Death of Europe: Immigration, Identity, Islam* (Bloomsbury, 2017).

long history. The doctrine of multiculturalism that displaced it dethroned the traditional culture and said, in effect, one is as good as another.

Guided by this defeatist ideology Europe's leaders have thrown open the doors to huge numbers of immigrants – many of them Muslim. Alongside this phenomenon there has been a demoralising loss of confidence in the value and worth of traditional European culture. Into this cultural vacuum a newly energised and vigorous Islam has moved to fill the space vacated. Already in Britain some of the practices of sharia law – that is the law code mandated by the Koran – are tolerated by the authorities. But now there are signs – predictably – of a backlash in some European countries as people wake up to the consequences of their leaders' decisions. This presages a difficult time ahead. Populist governments in Poland, Hungary and elsewhere have put down a marker saying, quite plainly, 'We do not want any more Muslim immigration'. The BBC abhors this stance and finds nothing positive to say about such governments; needless to say, it either ignores or vilifies any similar movements in Britain.

In this story of infiltration, cultural self-abasement and sur-render, the BBC has been deeply complicit. From the 1960s onwards the BBC's own culture turned against traditional British values which rested on a bedrock of Christian ideas. Liberalism, which rejects the idea of an objective morality, sequentially laid siege to aspects of that traditional morality that were enshrined in law and campaigned for new permissive legislation. This project was ultimately wholly successful; laws covering areas such as divorce, abortion and family rights generally are now fully aligned with dogmatic liberal diktat. Once social conservatism had been discredited and vanquished the BBC adopted the ideology of multiculturalism as its new core belief. Under this delusional, but rigorously enforced philosophy, critics of the new dispensation have been silenced through the simple expedient of not allowing them to be heard.

Scandalously, the BBC's foreign news coverage has been skewed to mask the true extent of Muslim aggression around the world. By any honest reckoning Christianity is now the most persecuted religion in the world. In the Middle East particularly, but in other regions also, some Christian communities which have existed nearly since the time of Christ himself have been driven to near extinction – but there is remarkably little reporting of this. Conflicts like those in Nigeria and the Philippines cannot be understood without explaining how an aggressive Muslim fundamentalism is driving them. The situations in the two countries have significant differences, but also an overarching similarity. In Nigeria, Muslims comprise about 50 per cent of the population, whereas in the Philippines only about 6 per cent of people are adherents of Islam; but in both countries militant jihadist groups – Boko Haram in Nigeria and the Moro Islamic Liberation Front in the Philippines – have used extreme violence in pursuit of the establishment of an Islamic republic. This is a familiar pattern from around the globe; Islamists, inspired by fundamentalist preachers who rely on Koranic injunctions for their authority, deploy murderous violence against non-Muslims. Unless the slaughter involves Westerners it often goes unreported, a phenomenon which has dismayed Christian leaders. Addressing the European Parliament in 2014, Pope Francis said:

> I cannot fail to recall the many instances of injustice and persecution which daily afflict religious minorities and Christians in particular. Communities and individuals today find themselves subjected to barbaric acts of violence: they are evicted from their homes and native lands, sold as slaves, killed, beheaded, crucified or burned alive, under the shameful and complicit silence of so many.

Who could he have been thinking of? The BBC has been shamefully silent and, hence, complicit, in this persecution. It is as though, even when it is innocent Christian communities that are being targeted, the BBC guards against allowing itself any hint of solidarity with those people. But when, as has happened in Burma, it is Muslims who are persecuted, the BBC devotes resources and scarce airtime to their plight. On the domestic front there are many aspects of Islam which should be held up to rigorous scrutiny, but the BBC simply refuses to allow this to happen. It has proved itself slow to investigate serious wrongs emanating from Muslim communities; it has done this because it will not allow any comparisons to be made which might show Islam to be in any way inferior to the Christian culture built up in these islands over two thousand years of history.

This refusal is rooted in a doctrinaire multiculturalism; an ideology which, though disavowed publicly in speeches by Tony Blair (2006) and David Cameron (2011), remains enthroned within the Corporation. The noble lie at the heart of this disastrous belief is that all cultures are deserving of equal respect and, even though people from these cultures come as strangers in our midst, they should be allowed to live according to their own lights. The truth is very different. The fact that modern Europe consists of a collection of humane and tolerant nation states is neither an accident, nor the result of some serendipitous cosmic good fortune; it is a consequence of Europe having adopted, centuries ago, Christianity as its creed. The values that modern liberals hold dear – even the delusions of multiculturalism – arise from the very philosophy they have worked so hard to de-legitimise and overturn. Islam – which earlier generations in Europe understood to be opposed to their own way of life – is now sheltered from proper critical scrutiny even as the fanatics that it inspires plot to kill us.

CHAPTER EIGHT

WHERE LIBERALISM LEADS – OR WHAT MARY WHITEHOUSE DIDN'T SEE COMING

IT WOULD BE EASIER to make a wholehearted defence of our culture in the face of the onslaught of Muslim fanatics if aspects of it were not so thoroughly corrupted. Nothing excuses the actions of jihadis who bomb, shoot or ram innocent civilians, but some of what is permitted in the name of liberal tolerance – a kind of 'pornogrification' – is very difficult to defend or justify. British social conservatives might easily be forgiven for feeling some sympathy for restrictive Muslim dress codes in the face of some of the current excesses. There is, for instance, a programme called *Naked Attraction*, which is now in its third season on Channel 4. The concept is a straightforward one: each week a young man or woman is asked to choose someone to date, not as in the conventional way according to personality and general attractiveness, but solely on how much they like the look of their genitals. This is how it works: the contestant stands centre stage, around which are situated six opaque glass boxes. In each box stands a naked man or woman. After an introduction by the presenter and a bit of banter the big moment comes; on cue the bottom half of each glass box rises up to waist height displaying for discussion and debate the genitals of each person. The contestant is led round and explains why he/she finds each set of genitals attractive ('very neat!') or unattractive ('too many tattoos!'). By a process of elimination the contestant then decides on one of the six to date.

This simple, if crude, formula has proved popular; every week it pulls in somewhere between 1.2 – 1.7 million viewers. According to one admiring industry website – WOW 24/7 – *Naked Attraction* is a 'cheeky TV series...' which 'stunned viewers' and consistently pulls in 'an impressive audience'. When it first aired in 2016 there was a short-lived stir of controversy; it drew some complaints and OFCOM investigated. It found that the programme hadn't breached any rules because it was just a type of dating show, and that there had been 'no sexual activity'.

The BBC has not yet stooped so low, but sexual titillation is a staple of its drama offerings, whether from its no-holds-barred comedy series *Fleabag*, to its 2018 hit series *Bodyguard*. There is a huge public appetite for shows which are sexy, and TV commissioning editors fully understand this, and act accordingly. A free society can choose what it will permit and what it will forbid and, it seems, contemporary Britain has made its choice. Whether that choice is fully informed or not is debatable; the fact that a show like *Naked Attraction* can be accorded the imprimatur of the industry regulator suggests that we are near reaching the point where any notion that some agreed standard of public decency will inhibit the broadcasters is clearly false. There was a time when it was supposed that television could, in part, be trusted to self-regulate; but *Naked Attraction* shows that the assumption that the broadcasters' own sense of self-restraint would act as a brake on the worst excesses has been shown to be wishful thinking.

People from the US television industry who come to Britain often remark that our broadcasters get far more leeway than they do in their own home market. They say that British viewers are exposed to much more swearing and sex than they could get away with in their mainstream shows. And many people, of course, celebrate this freedom, for it is an axiom of media liberals that restrictions are inherently a bad thing and that they should be allowed to get on with entertaining the public in whatever way the public enjoys. Which, naturally enough, includes shows where there is a lot of sex – because people like it. However, when a show like *Naked Attraction* is held up for scrutiny, what do we see? A programme which is coarse, cheapening, demeaning and exploitative; it is utterly devoid of cultural merit. It is demoralising and degenerate. But the culture which allows this goes virtually unchallenged; there are no voices any longer brave enough to say that this stuff corrodes public morals. Perhaps the fate of an earlier campaigner puts them off.

Mary Whitehouse is now a name known only to an older generation. She was a social activist who opposed what she saw as a lowering of moral standards in Britain, and her particular target was the television industry. Her campaigning life began in the 1960s when she founded the 'Clean up TV' campaign and then, in 1965 the organisation with which she became most identified, the National Viewers' and Listeners' Association (NVLA). From the outset she had the BBC in her sights; every programme which she judged to have breached standards of decency and good taste she complained about, and her campaigning was, to a limited extent, successful. At its peak the NVLA had the ear of government and she was able to lay her concerns before Harold Wilson's 1974 administration, though she got precious little action in return; Labour, then as now, has always been leery of social conservatism. In contrast, Mrs Thatcher was someone who instinctively sympathised with Mrs Whitehouse's campaign, but even during the Thatcher years Mary Whitehouse was never able to do much to stop the forward march of the permissive society.

Her problem was that she was battling against the spirit of

the age. Her moralising complaints made her the target of some quite vicious mockery. To her enemies she was a twentieth century incarnation of Mrs Grundy – the fictional prude in Thomas Moreton's 1798 play *Speed the Plough* – who embodies the tyranny of narrow-minded propriety. Though she was a doughty fighter for her beliefs, by the time she died in 2001 Mrs Whitehouse must surely have been aware that the culture war was lost. In every cultural sphere – art, music, literature, film – new, more permissive rules were put in place and artists took full advantage. The Old Order was in full retreat.

However, even she, I feel, could never have envisaged that mainstream British television would broadcast a literal genital beauty contest; *Naked Attraction* would have been beyond her worst nightmares, something unimaginable.

At the root of any objection to the kind of obsessive prurience on which the programme is based, is an anxiety of how it might change attitudes to human sexuality and thus affect our relationships. The commodification of sex, whether via outright pornography written or visual, or via a show like *Naked Attraction*, which is only 'milder' in the sense that no actual sex is shown, is a process we have learned to live with. The liberal says, 'Get over it, sex is a healthy human activity, what's not to like?'; the social conservative, conversely, sees sex reduced to transactional basics, stripped of beauty, grace or higher meaning and stripped also of some essential decency, which is part of what separates us from the beasts.

There is an enduring mystery as to why there has been so little opposition to this process, and the answer lies in the way in which public debate is channelled by the media. All politicians nowadays have to appeal to the centre ground of politics and, currently, the centre ground could not seem to care less about messages calling for self-restraint and even less for actual restrictions that might curb or ban outright material judged indecent. Because such objections are so rarely heard, it takes a brave soul to challenge the consensus. Most politicians are cowed by the thought of espousing any such policy – knowing that if they do so, they will immediately make influential enemies in the media. Social conservatives, when they break cover, as sometimes they do, face mockery and scorn; socially conservative views are apt to be labelled 'extreme', merely because they run counter to the prevailing commercial interests of the dominant media.

There is a theory, popular with some on the right, about the demise of social conservatism in Britain over the past thirty years. According to its adherents, Mrs Thatcher's government was the last Tory administration to offer any meaningful opposition to a liberal intellectual hegemony. There was, for instance, Section 28 of the Local Government Act 1988, which was aimed at preventing the promotion of homosexuality by local authorities. In particular it covered schools where the aim was to stop homosexuality being promoted as a 'pretended family relationship'. Whether the legislation accomplished any of its aims is unknown, but what it certainly did do was to give opponents a focal point around which they could rally. The agitation against Section 28 grew in volume in the following years. Spearheaded by gay rights groups, the protests were sustained for a decade and more until, in 2003, a new Local Government Act swept Section 28 away.

As a postscript to this, Tory-controlled Kent County Council tried to carry on with a provision of its own, which laid down that in its schools, children would be taught that heterosexual marriage and family relationships are the only firm basis for society. Eventually this local resistance, too, was squashed in 2010 when Harriet Harman guided the Equality Act onto the statute book. And so ended opposition to an idea rooted in a simple belief that traditional heterosexual family life is the ideal and, moreover, the best way of nurturing and raising children. Here is what the former Tory MP, now life peer, Dame Jill Knight said about why she campaigned in favour of Section 28:

I was contacted by parents who strongly objected to their children at school being encouraged into homosexuality and being taught that a normal family with mummy and daddy was outdated. To add insult to injury, they were infuriated that it was their money, paid over as council tax, which was being used for this. This all happened after pressure from the Gay Liberation Front. At the time I took the trouble to refer to their manifesto which clearly stated: 'We fight for something more than reform. We must aim for the abolition of the family.' That was what was going on and was precisely what Section 28 stopped.[1]

After Mrs Thatcher's overthrow came John Major, who led the country for seven years. His one notable sortie into social conservative territory came with the 'back to basics' drive which ended in mockery and fiasco. Launched by Major in a speech in 1993, 'back to basics' sought to promote traditional values like 'neighbourliness, decency and courtesy', but the initiative was torn to pieces in a media feeding frenzy. Spearheaded by the Murdoch press in particular, scandal after scandal involving Conservative politicians was uncovered, and by the end of Major's term in 1997 the Tories, in the popular mind at least, had no vestige of moral authority left.

Then came the Blair years, a period when, untrammelled by any meaningful opposition, New Labour drove the social liberal revolution forward. Some social conservatives believe that alongside New Labour's antagonism to the traditional family, its headlong championing of every socially liberal cause is its most dangerous legacy. The *Mail on Sunday* columnist Peter Hitchens, one of the very few prominent public voices of social conservatism, labels the Blairites 'Bolsheviks' – people who were

---

1 Dame Jill Knight, Hansard, 6 December 1999.

intent on destroying the traditional family and replacing it with something more attuned to 'inclusivity'. Under this thinking, each and every variation of family – be it homosexual or not, married or not – is accorded equal respect and legal standing.

When the Blair years ended and David Cameron's coalition government took over in 2010 the baton passed smoothly from one set of social liberals to another. In a dramatic move to bolster his credentials as a progressive, Cameron selected the legalisation of homosexual marriage as a totem. The legislation to permit same-sex marriage was passed in 2013, putting the UK at the forefront of a worldwide movement to confer parity of esteem on same-sex partnerships. By this point it could be argued that Britain had lost touch with the preceding generation's idea of 'normal'. The country had a 'new normal', which embraced types of relationships previously regarded as irregular.

To many fair-minded people these changes signal progress; they sincerely believe that all these changes, in what we consider decent, right and proper, are for the good. They think it signals that the country has thrown off the burden of a repressive and outdated morality. Social conservatives, conversely, believe that this new tolerance has gone too far and that, while it is a good thing that gay people are no longer persecuted, the traditional family is, and will always remain, the essential building block of a stable society. To that end, they argue, the state should do all in its power to bolster and sustain family life.

The culture war in Britain is rarely depicted in this way – the very idea that Britain has had a culture war is a foreign concept to many. But that is partly because the social liberals, who were the ones waging the war, were always at pains to disguise what their true aims were, or how transformational their ambitions. Each change, each step taken towards dismantling the old morality, came dressed in soft words, claiming that the old rules were unfair and discriminatory. The pitch was always made in the name of some group of supposed victims and the country, good-natured as always (because there is an underlying kindness in English society), went along with it. The qualms of the old guard were ignored and bypassed until it seemed to the casual observer that they had nothing much to say on the matter. The culture war had been waged and the social liberals won.

What has happened in Britain is all our own doing; there is no EU angle in the story of how social liberals won every argument from the 1960s onwards. In fact, other European countries have proved much slower to embrace this brave new world, and a minority has recently even tried to reverse the process. Hungary, under its leader Viktor Orbán, is the prime example of this – which is why he has become another *bête noire* of the British media. The BBC in particular shows little interest in reporting Mr Orbán fairly; the people who voted for him are merely dismissed as 'conservatives' – BBC shorthand for bad, unenlightened people. The ire of liberals is understandable: Orbán has quite explicitly made social conservatism a central plank of his political programme. In addition to his populist opposition to any further Muslim immigration – which is couched in terms of saving Europe's Christian heritage – Mr Orbán puts family-friendly policies centre stage. In May 2018, talking on state radio Orbán said: 'There are many kinds of families, many ways of life and it (liberal democracy) says we should not differentiate between these ... it wants to ensure equal treatment in the law.' He said that from the present day to 2030 Hungary, and Europe, should be defined by a modernised concept of Christian democracy: 'Christian democracy protects us from migration, defends the borders, supports the traditional family model of one man, one woman, considers the protection of our Christian culture as a natural thing.'

Orbán's forthright stance has led to a bitter stand-off with other EU members who oppose his stance on immigration (he is essentially against it) and family values. His opponents managed to engineer a vote in the European Parliament in September 2018 which, for the first time ever, passed a motion under Article 7 of the EU's constitution – a move which set in motion a process that could, eventually, lead to Hungary losing its voting rights in the bloc. Mr Orbán, who had just won a third handsome election victory, seems intent on sticking to his course. What he demonstrates is that the onward march of liberal values is not inevitable. People, and whole countries, can make choices which can alter the direction of travel. The contempt which the liberal-left in Britain holds for the likes of Orbán and Trump, is because both men are offering a challenge to an international liberal elite that sincerely believes in the rightness of its cause and the inevitability of its triumph.

September 2018 was notable, in a small way, for another reason: it marked the 175th anniversary of the foundation of *The Economist*. To mark the occasion its editor, Zanny Minton Beddoes, penned a 10,000-word essay entitled 'Reinventing liberalism for the 21st century'. Most of what she wrote could have been predicted by any regular reader of the magazine: there was a stout and well-argued defence of free trade, free markets, mass migration and limited government, combined with a call to arms to liberals everywhere to refine and re-energise liberalism which, in Minton Beddoes's view, is under unprecedented attack. But it was what she didn't say that was, in a way, most striking. There was no mention anywhere of the challenge that Islam poses to liberal democracies. This seems a serious omission given that one of the factors behind the growing resistance to immigration in many countries is the fear of militant Islam and the risk of allowing terrorists entry alongside peaceable migrants. There was also no mention of the moral dimension of liberalism.

This is something worth serious consideration. 'Liberalism' is an omnibus term; applied to economics it means one thing, applied to ethics and morals it means another. It is also a word which comes freighted with different nuances in different countries: in American political discourse, for instance, 'liberal' denotes a left-winger, whereas in Britain it does not. Conversely, many British 'liberals' are not enthusiastic about liberal economics, but very keen on permissive social policies. This leads to much confusion when discussing the issue. Zanny Minton Beddoes gets around this by affirming that 'liberalism is a broad faith' and, by couching it in credal terms, she raises an intriguing question: do social liberalism and economic liberalism always come as a package? Or, the question can be put in this way: if I am a liberal in economic terms, a believer in free trade and free markets, does that also mean I must believe in abortion, easy divorce and freely available pornography? When put in these terms the answer seems clear enough: no, it does not. It is perfectly possible to be a liberal in classical economic terms and yet be a social conservative. The two things are not inevitably conjoined, they do not walk in lockstep.

Here is an important clue to understanding what has happened in Britain in the past half-century. Liberalism has advanced on a broad front, which embraces both economics and morals. *The Economist* – a bellwether of liberal-elite opinion – always fights hard and argues cleverly for liberal economics, but takes liberal moral attitudes for granted. It rarely bothers to pronounce on moral issues, apparently assuming that its readers are of one mind. In contrast, the BBC is much less comfortable with liberal economics – one of the reasons why it was so opposed to Mrs Thatcher's economic policies – but is a fervent supporter of social liberalism. What the BBC and *The Economist* have in common is that they behave as if there is no real argument to be had about liberal social attitudes. What this betrays, aside from the narrow focus of those people who think that economic well-being is the only thing that really matters, is the hubris of social liberals. They really do believe the argument is over and that their side won it. But social conservatism is not dead; the political pendulum is always in motion and, just maybe, we are at the beginning of a long-overdue correction.

CHAPTER NINE

CONCLUSION: THE NOBLE LIE UNMASKED

A S WE SAW EARLIER, the noble lie was a concept originated by Greek philosopher Plato in the *Republic*. In it, Plato
imagines an ideal city state, and he contemplates how the people
of that state can stay united, despite the fact that there are stark
differences between the classes; at the top were to be the rulers
and then various other groups in descending order of social
status. Plato wonders about a question which remains relevant
in every modern society – how can everyone be kept happy:
why should the proles at the base of the social pyramid support
the established order, given that it condemns them to a life of
tough labour while the rulers live in luxury? A good question.
Plato's answer is to promote a foundation myth which explains

that the city's original human inhabitants had either some gold or some base metal added to their make-up. Those lucky ones who got the gold were the aristocrats, but the majority who got a dash of iron or lead ended up as the proles. And by this method, your station in life was a settled thing not, usually, to be changed. What is more, this story of the city's foundation would stress that all inhabitants come from the same root stock; in the beginning there was a common parentage and the descendants would thus be bound together by ties of blood and family even when their social status differed. So this 'noble lie' was a device to keep everyone committed to a common purpose. It was a myth with a purpose, the purpose being social harmony.

Things have moved on a bit since Plato's time but the problems our rulers face, in essence, have not. The first and most important task in any demos is to maintain social harmony. And, as Plato foresaw, sometimes to do that it will be necessary for those in charge to promote a myth – a 'noble lie' – to keep the peace. The 'nobility' of such a stratagem lies in its purpose; most people would agree, *a priori*, that it is better to tell the truth than to lie. But if the lie is told for some 'higher purpose', if for instance, it is told to promote good community relations, then it is possible to argue that the lie is necessary and the decision to tell it justified. This book is an attempt to pick apart some of the 'noble lies' that underpin British society; and it also offers a counter narrative to explain why those lies are neither noble nor necessary.

The bulk of this book has focused on the BBC and some people might think that it is unfair to do so. The BBC, it might be argued, is not alone in bending the truth to fit its own ideological stance; in fact, they would say, other media – newspapers, internet sites, other broadcasters – do far worse. There might be truth in that, but it also misses the point. The fact is that the BBC is unlike every other media organisation in the country. It is the 'national broadcaster', which must, by solemn promises underwritten in its charter, act differently from newspapers and other media. It is not allowed to take sides, although (as I have tried to demonstrate) it consistently breaches this obligation. So however much we might individually value the BBC, it can't be allowed to escape close scrutiny simply because it does a better job than some other media. Personally I support the BBC, which might seem paradoxical given the criticisms I make of it, but my reasoning is simple enough; firstly, if the BBC was abolished, any replacement is unlikely to be an improvement, and secondly, the fact that it is a public corporation with an explicit commitment to impartiality makes it, theoretically at least, susceptible to public pressure. The BBC's claim to be 'impartial' may raise a hollow laugh, but at least its critics can try to hold it to the standard it so proudly claims – even while it falls so far short.

There is a solemn covenant that lies at the heart of the BBC's relationship with the country, and it is this: in return for the licence fee revenue (a valuable privilege), it promises to tell the truth and to be impartial on all matters of public debate. This promise is broken on a daily basis and, over time, its performance is worsening. The BBC's world view, its composite 'noble lie', if you will, has become more pronounced, more dogmatic, more entrenched. On certain topics it barely tries to disguise its own prejudices any longer. Whether through carelessness or hubris it hardly even attempts to maintain the pretence of impartiality.

When President Trump was merely 'Candidate Trump' on the campaign trail, he hammered home one message in particular; he turned on the mainstream US media and accused it of peddling 'fake news'. As anyone who has had any experience of US journalists will know, they do not, as a group, lack self-esteem; on the contrary, American media folk are monumentally self-important. Trump's assault on their profession was bitterly resented and dismissed as the words of an inveterate liar who lacked the righteous virtues they see themselves possessing. The enmity between Trump and almost the entire Washington press corps set the scene for a confrontation the like of which we have not witnessed before.

The media in the US – and to a certain extent this differentiates it from its UK equivalent – puts an almost fetishist emphasis on factual accuracy in all things. Which is why many US media outfits employ 'fact-checkers'; these people are not journalists as such (though some of them hope to graduate to the status of reporter etc.), but their job is to ensure that factual mistakes don't slip through. So when Trump laid his charge against the likes of the *New York Times* – the pre-eminent liberal-left American newspaper – it could retort that it scrupulously checked all its facts before printing them. So, by its own estimation, it had refuted Trump's calumny. Fake news? Not guilty.

There were individual instances in this saga when the media won the point; Trump's vainglorious assertion that his inauguration had been the best attended in US history was proved wrong by press photos showing that was obviously not the case. But – and here's the point – proving the President wrong on instances like that in no way undermined his charge of 'fake news'. Trump wasn't saying that the press and the TV networks were getting the facts wrong, rather, they were telling the wrong stories. And Trump had a good point: it's a question of fairness, not facts. A report can be accurate and still deeply unfair whether by selection or omission. 'Fake news' is not so much about factual inaccuracy as about ideological bias; there are 'alternative truths' depending on the standpoint of the individual.

If Trump were a different kind of man with more intellectual pretensions he might have talked about 'ideological bias', but his genius is for communicating with the crowd and 'fake news' does the job; his supporters absolutely understood what he was saying because they too have learned not to trust the mainstream media. As in Britain, the US media is dominated by condescending liberals who look down on many of the concerns and beliefs of 'ordinary' people. The noble lie is far from being an exclusively British phenomenon.

None of the US networks (with the exception of the Trump-supporting, Murdoch-owned Fox News) were on Trump's side; they felt themselves to be his opponents and so consistently chose to run negative stories about him. These might have been (and almost certainly were, given the media's scrupulous checking) accurate, in a narrow sense, while at the same time being deeply partisan. Trump and his supporters knew this, hence his repeated attacks. And in case anyone thinks he was delusional, this bias towards the Democrats among US journalists has long been an established fact.

When Barack Obama addressed his first White House correspondents' dinner in 2009 he quipped: 'Most of you covered me, all of you voted for me'. It is an open secret that the US press corps overwhelmingly votes Democrat. When Trump faces the press he faces the enemy. And what about the BBC? After all, didn't Britain have a dog in the fight – surely the BBC could afford to be, indeed had a duty to be, impartial towards Trump and even-handed in its treatment of US politics? The BBC chewed over the 'fake news' issue at great length; there were discussions on all the heavyweight current affairs shows; an entire edition of *Start the Week* on Radio 4 was devoted to it with much talk about how we had entered into a 'post-truth' age where there were now 'alternative facts'.

The BBC's coverage portrayed Trump's attacks as evidence of his essential dishonesty and yet, throughout it all, it was striking the way in which the BBC utterly failed to understand how it is that many people see its own output on so many issues qualifying as 'fake news'. 'Fake' because it is deeply partisan and unfair and marginalises, or excludes, viewpoints that don't conform to its own belief system. The BBC is a highly professional organisation; its journalists are very good at what they do, and it is not often that they actually get the facts wrong. The BBC's fakery is all about bias – it's not about outright falsehoods.

It is one of the ironies of life in modern Britain that people who think of themselves as liberal are often deeply intolerant of the views of social conservatives; the new ruling class belong to a strange new category the 'liberal bigot'. A true liberal is one who is prepared to tolerate the views of others, but these bigoted liberals are prepared to tolerate only those views they agree with. In private life that doesn't matter much, but in the context of the BBC it matters a great deal. What it means is that there are certain views which the BBC will not allow to be aired. In some instances this is understandable and right; we do not want to see and hear from people so prejudiced that their views are an incitement to the hatred of others. But, whereas in theory, this is an easy category of argument to spot, in practice, it is not so.

The problem is well illustrated by a famous incident which occurred during the 2010 general election campaign when the

Labour leader, Gordon Brown, coming away from canvassing a voter, and forgetting that he still had a microphone attached, spoke of her as 'bigoted'. Her crime, in Brown's book, was to have raised the subject of immigration. Note the word raised; she had not indulged in a racist rant she had merely, in the course of a three-minute exchange, questioned the number of immigrants coming into her home town of Rochdale. But that was enough to damn her in Brown's eyes. It is this attitude – that some subjects are off-limits because to raise them at all automatically convicts you of the charge that you are 'bigoted' – that has so damaged public debate in Britain. And not just the debate – words matter – they change the world.

As Lord Patten is quoted as saying in an earlier chapter, he does not deny that the media has an effect on how society sees itself, although that doesn't seem much of an admission. One might wonder that anyone could seek to deny that the media have influenced society, which seems a banal observation, but is actually a statement of an obvious truth. But some people do take issue with the idea, especially when it is in the context of any discussion about bias in the media. The point is that if it were the case that what the BBC (or any other media outfit) says had no effect on society, then it really wouldn't matter a bean if the organisation was run by Marxists, or fascists for that matter. But if once you allow that what the organisation says does have an effect, then it begins to matter a great deal. The BBC is not some virtual mirror that society holds up and sees itself reflected back; a mirror changes nothing – it merely shows us what we look like. The BBC far more resembles a preacher; a good preacher does hold up a mirror to people and says, 'Look, this is who you are', but who then goes on to say, 'And this is what you should be'. And it is the BBC's role as preacher that we need to be aware of and to closely examine.

Margaret Hodge spoke no less than the truth when she said in 2007 that migration had for years been a taboo subject for fear of encouraging racism. But Ms Hodge is a politician – a senior Labour figure – and she is, of course, entitled, along with her party – to make any subject she wishes a personal 'taboo' for reasons of political calculation (Labour is relaxed about mass immigration, but knows it is not popular, so it suits the party to enforce silence on the issue). The interesting question is how is the taboo to be enforced? Given the unpopularity of mass immigration, why didn't the Conservatives force the issue into the open and make a pitch for votes on a platform of restricting and reducing immigration? It might seem like an obvious election platform. Until the last few years this never happened because they couldn't break the taboo. Whenever the issue was raised by the Tories it rebounded on them; and the reason that happened was because the BBC was ever vigilant in enforcing the ban.

For decades the BBC made sure there was to be the minimum debate possible surrounding immigrant numbers, and immigrant bad behaviour – or at least if such discussions did happen (which wasn't very often) the BBC would ensure that the charge of racism would be laid at the door of the dissenter. Enoch Powell, with his foolishly lurid rhetoric, made it all too easy for those people who favoured unfettered immigration; in fact, Powell and his 'rivers of blood' passed into journalese as shorthand for the supposed 'racism' of the right. This was such an effective tactic – few modern British politicians survive once convicted of the deadly charge – that a vital debate was never had.

Immigration is not an evil, immigrants are not bad people, healthy societies allow people in; all this is true. But it is one of the responsibilities of government to control the flow of immigrants – no government, or society, can afford to be entirely laissez-faire about who comes to settle in the country. For many decades, but particularly in the New Labour years, there was a deliberate policy to allow millions of newcomers and never to talk about it. The BBC was complicit in this arrangement because the people who work in the BBC agreed with New Labour and agreed with the rightness of the taboo. Things have changed over the past decade – now debate on immigration is tolerated (though not encouraged: the BBC does its level best not to highlight immigrant numbers); but the taboo has not shifted, at all, when it comes to discussions about any negative aspects of immigration. The BBC still makes sure that no link is established in the public mind between immigration and the housing shortage – obvious though that link is. Lord Patten, and liberals like him, think this is all for the best – and given the BBC's wholehearted agreement, that is not a view we are likely to see under sustained public challenge any time soon.

The process by which a society changes is a kind of alchemy; we tend not to notice it because we are part of the process. It is very difficult to put what's happening into focus when you are living through the change; we cannot see the wood, because we are the trees – the big picture is lost. We must look to historians to do the job at a later stage. History is a rear-view mirror, and when the time comes to explain what has happened in Britain in the years since the Second World War, the job of some historian of genius will be to dissect and explain the cultural revolution that has re-made Britain.

Right up until the 1960s it was a largely socially conservative country which acknowledged, and accepted, if somewhat grudgingly, a moral code based on Christian precepts that placed heavy emphasis on duty, self-restraint and personal discipline; the traditional family was recognised as the cornerstone of society and was rightly respected and celebrated. The new moralists challenged the old order with a seductive offer which said, in effect, 'We do not need these old, irksome restrictions; you are free to make your own decisions.' Britain thus became an experiment in an unfettered liberalism which, in a few short years, vanquished the old code and put in its place a philosophy which teaches that the highest good is each individual's personal fulfilment. The old moral code was vilified as repressive and out of date; young people were taught to rebel against discipline both at school and in the family.

Unsurprisingly, this turned out to be a wildly popular platform of reform. It is not difficult to persuade people, especially young people, that discipline is an unfair restriction on their personal liberty. How much more consoling to hear a message that what is right, is to do exactly what they want – especially in relation to the conduct of their personal lives. We are all selfish by instinct. The devil worshipper and charlatan Aleister Crowley, in his gobbledegook *Book of the Law*, condenses this down to a useful one-liner: 'Do what thou wilt shall be the whole of the Law.' Of course Britain still has laws and they do, to some extent, constrain personal conduct – but, crucially, not in those areas which are concerned with intimate personal conduct and sexual morality. In those areas personal preference is enthroned and this has, among other things, done colossal damage to family life.

It is important to recognise that the problems which preoccupy the media today are problems which the new morality has created. When the media frets – as it increasingly does – about the mental health of young people, the search for an explanation involves the usual suspects. The one currently in vogue is social media and the damaging pressure it can sometimes generate leading to feelings of inadequacy and worthlessness. What is almost never fingered as the culprit is divorce and family breakdown – although decades of academic inquiry have established beyond reasonable doubt that this is the single most important factor in determining a child's happiness. The reason why this discussion is rarely had is because opening it up would inevitably raise the question of whether society should do something to prop up stable families. This, in turn, would involve talking about how to make marriage more popular and divorce more difficult for people with children (the childless, it might be argued, are peripheral to this debate). Taken to its conclusion, this would mean re-instituting the taboo about divorce; society would have to be brought once again to the point where people disapproved of marital break-ups.

Suppose that such a discussion had 'wind in its sails' – by which I mean, suppose that the media got behind the idea and promoted a debate – then you might have the beginnings of a campaign which might, eventually, result in a change in the law. That would, in time, bring about change in society itself – to the benefit of future generations of children. But you, the reader, will immediately see why this cannot and will not happen while the current orthodoxy holds. The media – and the BBC in particular – has no interest in promoting such a debate because it offends against all its core beliefs about how society should operate. It would offend libertarians who object to anything which can be labelled 'judgemental' (that is anything which, according to an objective morality can be labelled 'right' or 'wrong'), and it would enrage feminists who would see it as an assault upon the sacred prerogatives of 'empowered' women to do exactly as they please. For, as long as these considerations remain the guiding principles of our culture, the needs of our children will be secondary to our determination to live as we please.

Or take another issue – the level of crime in society. If you go back sixty-five years and look at the crime statistics they are astonishingly low – astonishing, that is, by today's standards. In 1950 'total recorded crime' in England and Wales stood at 461,435 incidents; fifty years later in 2001, that number had risen to 5,525,024 – a greater than eleven-fold increase.[1] And the depressing truth is that the later figure probably underestimates the true level of criminality, because things that were once reported to the police and recorded by them are no longer consistently recorded. People have adjusted to a higher level of crime and also assume that the overstretched police force will do nothing about their complaint anyway. The clear-up rate for minor crimes like robbery and burglary are now pathetically low – 3 per cent in 2018 – and people know this is so which means that increasingly people have lost faith in the police.

You might think that seeking an explanation for this striking increase in crime is a question worth asking – though it

---

1 See UK government historical crime data: https://www.gov.uk/government/statistics/historical-crime-data

rarely is. Once again to do so would be to question the efficacy of the new morality in constraining criminal behaviour. The old morality was rather good at that; it induced a sense of guilt and there was public support for the condign punishment of offenders. The new morality weakens the stigma against criminality often by seeking to exculpate offenders by referencing the disadvantages of their circumstance. So it is that criminals become 'victims'. It would be simplistic to suggest that it was the BBC, single-handedly, that deposed the old morality, because the rest of the mainstream media in Britain enthusiastically joined in the demolition job.

The red tops like *The Sun* and the *Daily Mirror* used sex in a very obvious way to increase sales, while the newspapers with higher intellectual pretensions did the same job without the topless women. On moral questions like divorce, abortion and sexual conduct in general, it would be very hard to distinguish between the stance taken by say *The Times* and *The Guardian*, although there are differences of emphasis: *The Guardian* has campaigned vigorously for decades to ensure that no sexual practice should ever be deemed deviant, while *The Times* – true to form – has merely followed in the wake of changing fashion: where the establishment goes the Thunderer follows. Meanwhile, the *Daily Telegraph* has sometimes fought a lonely rear-guard action in defence of social conservatism with the *Daily Mail* sometimes in support; but they have not been able to stem the tide. None of the magazines which consider themselves as 'serious' could be considered as socially conservative with some – like *The Economist* – quite militantly liberal. As for the other broadcasters, none of them departs from the lead taken by the BBC, with Channel 4 somewhat ahead of the field in the race to be the most 'daring' (which is to say, transgressive).

All of this is merely to point out the obvious, which is that the media in all its various forms feeds off itself; where one takes the lead others follow and in this process it would be a mistake to underestimate the BBC's importance, which reflects its centrality in the British media landscape and the wider culture. It is difficult now to recall the excitement that once surrounded television in the 1960s; today it is something humdrum, even boring, and taken completely for granted, but back then it was glamorous and novel. Television in the '60s and '70s was the most desirable place to work for a whole generation of graduates, and the BBC, then as now the dominant organisation in the British media, was the employer of choice for the best and brightest of them. It was that intake of clever, well-educated young people, itching to put their own stamp on the world, who were at the forefront of the revolution. What they had in their sights was a set of moral strictures about personal conduct that they viewed as stale, fuddy-duddy and anachronistic. People still talk about the 'sexual revolution' of the 1960s, and sexual morality was at the heart of the momentous change that was then just beginning, but which has now become normative.

CONCLUSION: THE NOBLE LIE UNMASKED

To a large extent the liberal morality that now holds sway in Britain was the creation of the media age; it is 'media morality'. What you see on your screens, what you hear on your radio and read in your newspapers and magazines is the morality of media people. Whereas once adultery, promiscuity, drug taking, divorce and illegitimacy were not served up by the BBC on the grounds of protecting public morals, today these behaviours are the staples of its dramas and soap-operas. That this should be so is not surprising, but nor was it inevitable. The reason being that the advent of television moved influence away from traditional authority figures and exposed the whole population to a quite different set of values ordained by the broadcasters. And, as public behaviour, influenced by a permissive media changed, the broadcasters were ever quick to argue that what they showed on the screen merely 'reflected real life'.

Media people favoured the new rules that were far more permissive than the old ones. But this process was not inevitable: had that '60s intake of graduates been socially conservative in outlook, events might have taken a different course. There was something that happened in the '40s, '50s and '60s in education, particularly in universities, that loosened the grip of Christianity. As C. S. Lewis's brother discovered, even in the 1940s Oxford dons were strikingly hostile to religious belief; today the Academy is wholly dominated by an atheistic rationalism that goes unchallenged in the media.

Liberals assume that the more tolerant a society is the better it will be; like money, tolerance is supposedly something you can never have too much of. But multiculturalism, which was supposed to be the policy vehicle leading us towards a more tolerant future, gives the lie to this. Multiculturalism was sold to the British public as the natural and proper outcome of traditional British tolerance; we were told that we should not, as the host population, expect immigrants to conform to our culture and to integrate with it. To expect these strangers to do that, we were told, was intolerant, and what in part distinguishes multiculturalism is the absence of emphasis put on the need for integration. Instead, we should encourage immigrants to bring with them the culture of the homelands they had left behind. Britain was to become a 'community of communities', and all their cultures were to be held in equal esteem with our own. When the consequences of this disastrous approach started to become apparent, some of its former champions rowed back; Prime Ministers Blair and Cameron both, eventually, disowned the whole idea, but despite their renunciations multicultural-ism remains enthroned in the BBC's thinking.

What this means is that every news story, every documentary, every drama and soap opera has to pass a multicultural test; will this show a minority group in a bad light? If the answer is 'yes', it fails the test and doesn't make it onto the airwaves. The practical effect of this way of thinking is that real prob-lems and abuses are flourishing in the undergrowth of British society and the media spotlight carefully avoids highlighting them for fear of giving offence to one of the many immigrant communities. The most shocking example of this was the Muslim rape gangs which operated, with apparent impunity, for years, because everyone was too afraid of being accused of 'racism' to do or say anything about it. The penalty for breaking the silence on this subject remains severe; 'Tommy Robinson' (whose real name is Stephen Yaxley-Lennon) is a political activist who co-founded the English Defence League in response to what he sees as the takeover of British society by Islam. In May 2018 he was sentenced to thirteen months jail for contempt of court for trying to publicise details on an ongoing rape-gang trial at Leeds Crown Court. When they feel it is necessary, the authorities can play very rough in order to maintain the noble lie.

And there are other issues, too, which are being deliberately overlooked to avoid giving offence; the growth of polygamy, for instance. Polygamy is not recognised in Britain, which is to say that the law of the land allows a man to have one wife and a wife to have one husband; any person who has two wives or two husbands commits the crime of bigamy. But this law rests on the assumption that these spouses are acquired through an 'official' marriage – that is one registered with the appropriate authorities. Such a marriage has legal standing and confers rights and obligations on both parties. In Islamic tradition, on the other hand, a man can have up to four wives (a woman, by contrast, can only have one husband – this is definitely not a 'what's sauce for the goose...' culture), but these are contracted under sharia law – traditional Islamic jurisprudence which conforms to the edicts of the Koran. So there are a growing number of Muslim men in the country who take extra wives in this way; one of these wives might be 'official', whereas the others are recognised only according to sharia. Needless to say there are no accurate statistics about this phenomenon, but some estimates put the number of men who avail themselves of this arrangement at upward of 20,000. And the number is growing; a specialist website, secondwife.com, was founded a couple of years ago and does a brisk trade in Muslim men seeking extra wives.

Thus it is that polygamy – a practice forbidden by Christian tradition because it so obviously subordinates the female to the male – is gaining a foothold in Britain and is likely to be a growth area in the future. Under the diktats of multicultural theory this is not something that the rest of society should be worried about – 'it's a cultural thing' – but any woman contracted by sharia as a second, third or fourth wife is in a vulnerable position. She cannot avail herself of the ordinary protections offered to women under British law – those same laws that feminists have fought so hard to get onto the statute book. She would have no claim, in law, to any of her 'husband's' property for instance. Add to that the ease with which a Muslim man can divorce a wife under sharia and one can see just how exposed the position of any supernumerary wife is. The open question is whether contemporary British society has the will to try to curb polygamy; if it hasn't, which on current form seems highly likely, it might not be long before trade starts to flow in the other direction. My guess is that there are many non-Muslim men who might find the idea of their own little harem quite attractive. A situation wittily explored in Michel Houellebecq's disturbingly prescient novel *Submission*. In the final scenes of the book the central character, a dissolute bohemian academic, is seduced into collaborating with the new Islamic French government, partly by the enticing prospect of being able to take up to four young wives. For sexually voracious males Islam offers tempting inducements.[2]

It is a great irony that Islam is treated with kid gloves by the BBC and most of the rest of the British media because Islam is the embodiment of social conservatism *par excellence*. The social conservatism of Christianity pales in comparison with the kind of attitudes which are routine within Muslim communities. On those issues where media liberals have fought so ferociously to overturn supposedly harsh Christian attitudes – abortion, homosexuality, the role of women among them – Islam offers far more trenchant versions of the same. On homosexuality, for instance, the Koran is fiercely and unequivocally condemnatory, and no contemporary Islamic

2   Michel Houellebecq, *Submission* (William Heinemann, 2015).

authority has seen fit to temper this conviction. The New Testament, by comparison, offers no guidance on the subject, which suggests Christian attitudes to gay people should be governed by the same rules as apply to all other relationships: to love thy neighbour. That is why homosexual people who had the misfortune to fall under the sway of the Islamic State met such horrible deaths, thrown from high buildings or executed in other foul ways. And yet, militant British feminists are often to be heard defending Muslims against 'Islamophobia'. How can this contradiction be explained?

Kimberlé Williams Crenshaw's theory of intersectionality has the virtue of giving a name to a phenomenon which was long in evidence before she coined the word; the tendency in left-wing political movements to bring together apparently disparate causes under one roof. Intersectional feminism is the ideological omnibus which all the other causes of the left can clamber aboard. So it is that green agitators and LGBT activists all can find a seat on the big pink bus along with a whole host of campaigns which can be categorised as manifestations of identity politics. Conservative Muslims might seem to be the least likely of fellow travellers on the sisterhood's intersectional journey, but space has been made for them. Logic would suggest that feminists should find it much easier to make common cause with Christians because a true understanding of the Christian faith confers complete parity of worth on all men and women. But, in fact, the overthrow of the Christian faith as the *fons et origo* of Western values was always, and remains, feminism's goal – one which has now been, to all intents and purposes, achieved. So, while an outsider might wonder at the spectacle of feminists defending Islamic practices which clearly put women in a subordinate position, all is explained by feminism's hatred of traditional Christian morality.

Feminism is, of course, not a homogeneous movement and there are deep divisions within it; witness the contorted debate over transgender 'women' and the fierce disagreements between feminists on issues like pornography and prostitution. These divisions will not quickly be healed, but in the wider context they don't matter much because the main goal of feminism now is to maintain the intellectual hegemony already achieved. Nowhere is this dominance more firmly entrenched than at the BBC; the Corporation neither encourages, nor indeed allows, any serious challenge to feminist theorising; feminist philosophy is now so closely woven into the BBC's understanding of the world that it has become normative.

Tragically this is no recipe for harmony between the sexes, but for a never-ending war waged by feminism against men and masculinity. The BBC's noble lie in this regard is that feminism's advance is unfinished business whereas, in fact, its central precepts are now woven into the Corporation's world view. No challenge is ever made to radical feminism's central charge that women are oppressed by an oppressive patriarchy.

You might not hear it stated in quite those terms, but the starting point of any BBC discussion on issues involving women is that females have been, and still are, treated unfairly by a society weighted in favour of males. In public debate feminism has triumphed and, like the fish in the joke, young women today might fairly ask, 'What's feminism?' – it is the very water they swim in.

The problem is that continuing the feminist struggle can only worsen relations between men and women. The empowerment of women has come at the cost of a concomitant disempowerment of men. A humbled, patronised and increasingly resentful masculinity is unlikely to stay for ever quiescent as it sees its prerogatives dismantled and its virtues mocked. Fifty years ago there were real injustices and the grievances of womankind were rightly and properly addressed. What purpose there is today in continuing the fight has to be wondered at.

It is not well understood the extent to which the society we have created differs in an important, indeed fundamental way, from nearly all those that we know something about from history. For the first time in our species' long experience of living as social animals in cooperative communities we seem to have decided to dispense with a unifying, overarching idea of what we are, what we believe and what we aspire to be. In most examples that swim up from the murky historical depths, what a society was really about – its guiding philosophy

– is readily apparent; the Soviet Union, for instance, or the Ottoman Empire, or apartheid South Africa or the Japan of the Shogunate. In each one of these instances a reasonably well-informed person could make a stab at categorising the underlying philosophy that powered those societies. But faced with the Britain of today and asking the same question, what possible answer could there be?

One answer – though it seems wrong to dignify it with the label of a 'philosophy' – is materialism, the worship of money. All the main political parties believe in the idea that the country should always be getting richer in terms of simple material prosperity; there is a difference in emphasis with the left arguing for more redistribution, but there is no argument about the idea that a bigger economy and a richer country are good for everyone. This idea, the one that permeates every other political debate from Brexit to the NHS, means that there is a constant, neurotic focus on the nation's economic well-being. But it seems a truth almost too obvious to need stating that increasing affluence, even if it was equally shared by all, is not any kind of panacea. If the country gets to be 10 per cent richer in the next five years will we be 10 per cent happier? You have to be a materialist of a very primitive mindset to believe such a thing. Of course poverty doesn't make people happy – it is an evil – and there are powerful arguments in favour of bettering the lot of the poor, but for the rest of the population further marginal increases in prosperity are not going to make the population any happier. Human discontents and unhappiness will not be saved by an ever-rising GDP.

Fifty years ago one might have been able to say, with some justification, that Britain was a 'Christian country'; that claim would be very much harder to substantiate today because our laws no longer reflect Christian teaching in the way they once did. And yet it is also clear that many people, not necessarily practising Christians, have a residual attachment to the idea that the country is in some way Christian: a poll in 2018 found 73 per cent[3] of British respondents declared themselves to be Christian. Nevertheless, a common trope is that the country is now 'post-Christian'; but what does that actually mean? Certainly, formal Christian worship has dwindled and is now very much a minority pursuit but, as many commentators have also pointed out, the beliefs of the intellectual elite which they themselves often proudly classify as 'Enlightenment values' seem to draw upon a wellspring of Christian philosophy. It is difficult to imagine that without the Christian Church there could have been an Enlightenment. For centuries, Christianity in Europe

---

3 The Pew Research Center May 2018, see: http://www.pewforum.org/2018/05/29/being-christian-in-western-europe/. The survey asked respondents to self-identify their religious affiliation and found the 'most Christian' country to be Portugal (83 per cent) followed by Austria, Ireland and Italy (80 per cent). In France 64 per cent identified as Christian; Holland was the only country where a minority (41 per cent) call themselves Christian. In every country surveyed only a minority of people who call themselves Christian actually practised their religion.

nurtured the idea of human dignity and the inalienable right of the individual to inquire, to question and to think. There is nothing in Christian teaching which inhibits intellectual inquiry; one of the best-known biblical parables is the story about the use of talents: Christians are taught that putting their talents to use – whatever they are – is the righteous thing to do. Whatever its supposed faults, Christianity has always treasured and proved fertile ground for human creativity; one need only think of Michelangelo painting the Pope's ceiling or Shakespeare (who may well have been a believing Catholic) to see the truth of the observation. But if we are now, truly, in a post-Christian era, what will we put in its place? When one thinks of the ideas commonly used to hold a community together, which ones are applicable to contemporary Britain? There is no unifying religious idea; the shallow atheism and rapacious consumerism which seems to be the 'spirit of the age' is thin gruel, and unlikely to meet people's emotional and psychological needs – especially in the event of a real national crisis of some sort. Nationalism (of which Brexit is a symptom) certainly lurks under society's skin, but it is a hotly contested area and seems unsuitable – and perhaps rather frightening – as a unifier. Certainly the most militant of the Remain campaigners have been quick to demonise what they term 'English nationalism'. Here, for instance, is Will Hutton, formerly the BBC's *Newsnight* economics correspondent, now principal of Hertford College, Oxford, writing about Brexit in *The Guardian* in July 2018:

'This is now nakedly the cause of English nationalists, whose marginalisation requires the broadest of progressive coalitions. Call it, perhaps, a new popular front.'[4]

A 'broad popular front', which would have to do without the support, it seems, of 'English nationalists' who, one supposes, include a fair swathe of Middle England. This kind of lazy anti-English prejudice is likely only to antagonise people but, more to the point, underlines the perils of trying to harness nationalism as a unifying theme in a British context. There is no agreed nationalism in Britain, only competing nationalisms at odds with each other.

The dethroning of the old, serviceable Christian mores, in the name of secularisation was an act of unilateral moral disarmament that created a vacuum from which, as yet, no replacement has emerged. But nature, as every student of physics knows, abhors a vacuum, and the idea of a society without an agreed set of beliefs seems both unnatural and very probably unstable. The hope must be that some new and benign philosophy will emerge to which the population can all sign up. Perhaps 'all' is too great an ambition, but one might wish for at least sufficient numbers to represent a majority, or a big minority, that can act as agreed centre ground and which can carry the day.

---

4 Will Hutton, 'Progressives in Britain can still triumph if they look to Spain's success', *The Guardian*, 22 July 2018.

The BBC's candidate to fill the ideological vacuum, which it shares to a greater or lesser degree with the rest of the mainstream media, comprises four main elements. Firstly, an unquestioning support for economic policies that will generate further prosperity. Both the left and the right divide on how this should be achieved, but not with the central proposition that ever-increasing national wealth is the desired objective. Secondly, a wholehearted endorsement of radical feminism's analysis of society's ills. This makes the supposed 'patriarchy' the villain of the piece, but its principal weakness lies in its divisiveness; there will never be peace between the sexes as long as the feminist agenda is promoted. Thirdly, multiculturalism as a guiding principle in how British society should be organised. The problem with this is that it involves the constant denigration of the indigenous culture, and the elevation of incoming cultures to parity of esteem regardless of their faults. And, fourthly, a rigid adherence to the dictates of political correctness. Political correctness can be likened to the camp guards patrolling the perimeter wire to make sure dissidents are dealt with. It is the jack-booted enforcer who kicks dissenters into submission saying, 'You will tolerate what I say must be tolerated and condemn what I say must be condemned, and if you do not you will be branded racist or misogynist or Islamophobe and be shamed off the public stage.'

But, as I have tried to demonstrate, this ramshackle philosophy is both unfair and unworkable. It is thin stuff, enforced by dogmatic and self-righteous sectarians, which cannot nourish the deep yearning that human beings have for meaning. It is a noble lie, devised by the destroyers of the old morality, in the hope that it will keep the peace.

In the long run this inchoate philosophy – because of its divisiveness, arbitrariness, unfairness and sheer unnaturalness – will create a powerful coalition of losers (men, indigenous whites and social conservatives, among others) who will fight back. It is a set of ideas which runs counter to human nature and in place of a philosophy (Christianity) that is profound and deeply compassionate, substitutes a fashionable melange of modish prejudice. It is supported by only a small minority, but this is the minority that rules the country. But the ideas which unite them will never deliver true social harmony; in the long run their project is doomed to fail.

With no coherent replacement yet in sight the danger is that something else arises to fill the void which will be neither benign nor practical; it will be insufficient to carry the burden of our collective spiritual aspirations. Some on the militant wing of Islamic expansionism, talk of 'da'wah' – that is Islamic proselytisation – which they dream will conquer Europe and convert the hereditary Christian lands; however, it remains to be seen what the long-term impact of terrorist outrages done in Islam's name will be. On the face of it, cruel and bloody terrorism seems unlikely to win many converts other than a few disturbed and alienated souls.

In the meantime, the hope of our elite is that European Muslims will succumb to the corrosive effects of affluence and secularism; they might, they hope, in time become indistinguishable from their neighbours. There are reasons to doubt this, namely because Islam evokes such powerful loyalty in its adherents enforced by punishment for apostates. Unlike other major religions, Islam is as much a political as a purely spiritual system; it is difficult to see how Islam can coexist alongside a modern Western state freed from confessional bonds. In Islamic countries the law (sharia) flows directly from the Koran and this makes ceding power to a secular state, or even sharing power with it, deeply problematic.

The future is, as always, unknowable, and anyone who predicts how things will turn out risks embarrassing themselves. Although a committed Protestant himself, the sociologist Peter Berger writing in the *New York Times* in 1968 said, in a much-quoted article, that 'by the twenty-first century, religious believers are likely to be found only in small sects, huddled together to resist a worldwide secular culture.' It was a prediction enthusiastically taken up by liberal intellectuals in the US and Britain who yearned to dismantle the Christian foundations of their societies. The following three decades saw, among other things, an Iranian revolution in the name of Islam, the collapse of the atheistic Soviet Union triggered by Catholic resistance in Poland, and the emergence of a resurgent Hindu nationalism in India. As I write, violent

Islamism is proving a profoundly destabilising force across the globe. None of this was foreseen by Berger in the 1960s – a time when Western sociology had more or less written off religion – all religions – as a spent force destined to be of historical interest only. The secularist prediction was as hubristic then as it is now; the BBC, and others, find it hard to acknowledge the undeniable fact that religious belief continues to enlist the deepest loyalties of billions of people around the world.

Peter Berger eventually realised that the 'secularisation theory' – which predicted the withering away and eventual disappearance of religion altogether, had been hugely over-sold. Religion had made a comeback – in fact it had never been away. He was later to write that the popularity and influence of secularisation theory among the intellectual classes stem-med from:

> an international subculture composed of people with Western-type higher education … that is indeed secular-ized. This subculture is the principal 'carrier' of progressive, Enlightened beliefs and values. While its members are relatively thin on the ground they are very influential as they control the institutions that provide the 'official' definitions of reality, notably the educational system, the media of mass communication and the higher reaches of the legal system.

This is a precise description of contemporary British society where it is indeed true that the higher reaches of the media, the law, education and politics are dominated by exactly the type of people he describes. It is their power and influence which sustain the noble lies that shape our reality. In Britain the BBC is a critical part of the system, and uses its enormous influence to ensure its survival. It was hitherto the case that the BBC understood its duty to uphold and sustain the traditional – which is to say, Christian – culture of Britain. In 1934 the Corporation's governors decided to change its motto to a single word – 'Quaecunque' – meaning 'Whatsoever'. This was inspired by St Paul's Epistle to the Philippians:

> Finally brethren, whatsoever things are true, whatsoever things are honest, whatsoever things are just, whatsoever things are pure, whatsoever things are lovely, whatsoever things are of good report; if there be any virtue, and if there be any praise, think on these things. [4:8]

It was this text that inspired the inscription still to be seen in the old entrance foyer of Broadcasting House. It reads:

DEO OMNIPOTENTI TEMPLUM HOC ARTIUM ET MUSARUM ANNO DOMINI MCMXXXI RECTORE JOHANNI REITH PRIMI DEDICANT GUBERNATORES PRECANTES UT MESSEM BONAM BONA PROFERAT

SEMENTIS UT IMMUNDA OMNIA ET INIMICA PACI
EXPELLANTUR UT QUAECUNQUE PULCHRA SUNT
ET SINCERA QUACUNQUE BONAE FAMAE AD
HAEC AVREM INCLINANS POPULUS VIRTUTIS ET
SAPIENTIAE SEMITAM INSISTAT.

Which translates as:

This Temple of the Arts and Muses is dedicated to Almighty
God by the first Governors of Broadcasting House in the
year 1931, Sir John Reith being Director-General. It is
their prayer that good seed sown may bring forth a good
harvest, that all things hostile to peace or purity may be
banished from this house, and that the people, inclining
their ear to whatsoever things are beautiful and honest
and of good report, may tread the path of wisdom and
uprightness.

It was only in 1948 that the BBC changed its motto to 'Nation
shall speak peace unto nation'. In doing so, something had
been lost and it would be a fine thing if the BBC might, one
day, be prompted to recall that earlier dedication; the country
would be the better for it. However, for all that the BBC and
the intellectual class ignore and belittle religion – especially
the Christian religion – it is certain that as long as there are
human beings, there will be religion.

So here is one prediction that I am comfortable making: society does not stand still and change will come.

Just look at the Brexit vote. For many years it seemed as if there was no prospect of ever breaking free from the EU, that corrupt, unloved and undemocratic behemoth. The forces arrayed in favour of it were formidable: the political class, the Academy, big business and big money and the BBC were all rooting for Brussels; the BBC's role was to keep the debate as muted as possible and, for many years, it succeeded. But, eventually, the establishment forces were defeated by a maverick band of sceptics urged on by a couple of influential newspapers. The fact is that in a democracy, you cannot forever deny the will of the people. The noble lie of Europe – that our destiny lay in a European superstate and we would all be better off and happier because of it – foundered in the face of a profound scepticism about the project. So while today, political correctness is rigidly enforced by the media and the law (via the 'hate crime' regulations among other things), it will not be so for ever. Remember Brexit and take heart.

Our current confusions, our lack of a unifying idea, our heedless pursuit of our own selfish interests, are the inevitable result of a culture which promotes individualism and material prosperity as the highest goods. This is the consequence of the triumph of a shallow rationalism in harness with a fashionable atheism; in this belief system science and money are supposed to provide the answer to all our problems, including to the most profound questions that lie at the heart of the mystery of human life. Our ruling elite in Britain – the politicians, lawyers, academics and media people – view the current state of affairs as a positive thing; 'We have banished superstition', they say, rejoicing at the thought; but there remains a sceptical minority who look at the society brought into being by this type of thinking and see little to admire. The liberal hegemony has created an unhappy society which doesn't really know what it believes in. And whether you are a supporter of the current orthodoxy or not, here is one certain thing you can rely on: it is not permanent. The qualities that made Christianity a force to be reckoned with – the truth that wins human hearts and compels belief – have not changed, and will go on winning converts to its banner. In the coming years, who is to say whether the old beliefs will not triumph again over the arid fictions of our current noble lie?

ABOUT THE AUTHOR

ROBIN AITKEN IS A FORMER BBC reporter and journalist who spent twenty-five years working across all levels within the Corporation, from local radio to the *Today* programme. He is the author of *Can We Trust the BBC?* (Continuum, 2007) and the co-founder of the Oxford Foodbank, for which he was awarded an MBE in 2014 in recognition of his work. He is married with two daughters and lives in Oxford.

INDEX

PAPERBACK, £9.99

2016 marked the birth of the post-truth era. Sophistry and spin have coloured politics since the dawn of time, but two shock events – the Brexit vote and Donald Trump's elevation to US President – heralded a departure into murkier territory.

From Trump denying video evidence of his own words, to the infamous Leave claims of £350 million for the NHS, politics has rarely seen so many stretching the truth with such impunity.

Bullshit gets you noticed. Bullshit makes you rich. Bullshit can even pave your way to the Oval Office.

This is bigger than fake news and bigger than social media. It's about the slow rise of a political, media and online infrastructure that has devalued truth.

This is the story of bullshit: what's being spread, who's spreading it, why it works – and what we can do to tackle it.

HARDBACK, £10

Contemporary art is obsessed with the politics of identity. Visit any contemporary gallery, museum or theatre, and chances are the art on offer will be principally concerned with race, gender, sexuality, power and privilege.

The quest for truth, freedom and the sacred has been thrust aside to make room for identity politics. Mystery, individuality and beauty are out; radical feminism, racial grievance and queer theory are in. The result is a drearily predictable culture and the narrowing of the space for creative self-expression and honest criticism.

Sohrab Ahmari's book is a passionate *cri de coeur* against this state of affairs. *The New Philistines* takes readers deep inside a cultural scene where all manner of ugly, inept art is celebrated so long as it toes the ideological line, and where the artistic glories of the Western world are revised and disfigured to fit the rigid doctrines of identity politics.

The degree of politicisation means that art no longer performs its historical function, as a mirror and repository of the human spirit — something that should alarm not just art lovers but anyone who cares about the future of liberal civilisation.

— **AVAILABLE FROM ALL GOOD BOOKSHOPS** —